NARCISSISTIC ABUSE RECOVERY

A WOMAN'S JOURNEY TO SELF-FORGIVENESS, LOVE,
RESILIENCE, HAPPINESS AND SUCCESS THROUGH
AFFIRMATIONS

DAPHNE RICE

TABLE OF CONTENTS

INTRODUCTION

> "When a toxic person can no longer control you, they will try to control how others see you. The misinformation will feel unfair, but you stay above it, trusting that other people will eventually see the truth just like you did."
>
> — *JILL BLAKEWAY*

Narcissistic abuse, particularly in intimate relationships, is alarmingly common yet often remains hidden in plain sight. Disturbingly, one in three people may find themselves in a relationship with someone exhibiting narcissistic behaviors at some point in their lives. These relationships often involve complex dynamics of domination, aggression, and control—patterns that are not restricted to any one gender, manifesting differently between males and females (Day et al., 2021).

For a long time, I couldn't admit to myself that my ex-husband was a narcissist. The realization came too late, amid a tumultuous divorce, the drained finances, the emotional toll, and the self-doubt about whether I would ever breathe freely again. Each email or text from him was a potential bomb, a barrage of words that often left me with severe reflux and nausea, a physical manifestation of the sheer terror and anxiety his communications evoked. The constant state of alert, waiting for the next horrible thing he would say or the next threat he would make—no one should have to live under such duress.

Narcissistic abuse, as you may know, is not just about obvious aggression. It's the covert emotional and psychological manipulations—gaslighting, the silent treatments, the public demeaning that are often masked by a façade of normalcy to the outside world. It's these daily battles that deplete you, making you question your reality and your sanity.

This book and its companion journal are designed to serve as your allies on a path to healing. They offer daily affirmations for empowerment, crafted to help rebuild your self-esteem, process grief, and foster forgiveness toward not only those who have hurt you but, most importantly, toward yourself. These affirmations are tools to transform your internal dialogue from one of self-doubt to one of strength and positivity.

I understand firsthand the tough road of healing. The traits of your toxic ex—whether they manifested as overt dominance or covert manipulation—can leave deep scars. This book is my love letter to my younger self and to you—

crafted from the heart of my experiences, offering a hand to hold through your journey of recovery. It aims to validate your feelings, acknowledge your struggles, and equip you with tools to reclaim your narrative. Each affirmation and exercise is a step toward recognizing your worth, establishing healthy boundaries, and gradually building a life defined not by your past but by your resilience and capacity to love yourself.

As you begin this emotional and life-changing journey, remember the importance of patience and self-compassion. Healing from narcissistic abuse is not a linear process; it is full of ups and downs. But with commitment and support, you can navigate this path and emerge stronger. I invite you now to open your heart and mind to the possibility of a healed, happy future. Embrace each day's affirmation as a stepping-stone toward a life where you feel empowered and truly valued.

1

UNVEILING NARCISSISM AND ITS MARKS ON THE SOUL

> *"The narcissist devours people, consumes their output, and casts the empty, writhing shells."*
>
> — *SAM VAKNIN*

I remember standing in the kitchen, sunlight filtering through the window, trying to steady my trembling hands as I read another email from my ex-husband. My daughters were laughing in the living room, blissfully unaware of the storm inside me. Each word I read felt like a jab, reopening old wounds and carving new ones. The emotional toll was heavy—I constantly doubted my reality and questioned my sanity. This emotional whirlwind was mentally exhausting and manifested physically, too. There were days when just the sound of a notification would trigger a wave of nausea so strong I had to steady myself and take deep breaths before I could even look at my phone.

This chapter, my friends, is born from those dark times. It's for anyone who's felt their stomach churn at the buzz of their phone, who's felt the sting of manipulation so subtly woven into their daily interactions that it became their norm. It's for you who've doubted your memories and judgments under the relentless pressure of a narcissist's influence.

Together, we'll start by uncovering the mechanisms of gaslighting and manipulation—how they distort your reality and erode your self-esteem. We'll explore the psychological and physical manifestations of such profound stress. From cognitive dissonance and chronic anxiety to the physiological responses that leave us drained, we'll lay everything bare.

We'll also discuss the specific challenges of parenting under these conditions. How do you maintain confidence in your decisions, protect your children, and rebuild a nurturing environment when doubt and fear have become your constant companions?

Financial and social isolation often follow in the shadow of such relationships. We'll navigate the difficult paths of regaining financial independence and reconnecting socially, constructing a safety net that holds us tight when we falter. And lastly, we'll address the silent suffering that happens behind closed doors, offering strategies to break the silence and begin healing in community. This chapter is a step toward turning our lived horrors into a fortress of strength and empowerment.

THE NARCISSIST'S PLAYBOOK: RECOGNIZING GASLIGHTING AND MANIPULATION

Imagine standing in a room painted in colors you've never seen, hearing whispers that no one else can hear, and feeling a cold that doesn't exist. That's what gaslighting can feel like —an ongoing assault on your reality that leaves you questioning everything, even your sanity.

Gaslighting, a cruel and subtle form of manipulation, plays out in ways that can often make you mistrust your memories, perceptions, and even your emotions (March et al., 2023). This method of psychological control is deeply rooted in the dynamics of power and manipulation, aiming to make you feel unstable and dependent.

The tactics are diverse and insidious. Imagine sharing a concern with someone you trust, only to be met with outright denial or being told, "That never happened." Over time, this repeated denial makes you question your reality. You might recall a conversation vividly, but the gaslighter will deny it ever occurred, or they might trivially dismiss your feelings, suggesting you're too sensitive or overreacting.

A common tactic is the use of **lying and contradiction**. One day, they shower you with affirmations, and the next day, they flatly contradict themselves, denying they ever said such things. This continuous inconsistency shakes the foundation of your reality, making it nearly impossible to know what or whom to believe.

Guilt-tripping is another powerful tool in the gaslighter's arsenal, crafted to erode your sense of agency and foster an environment of self-doubt. This is often deployed to manipulate you into feeling responsible for the gaslighter's emotions or circumstances, regardless of the reality. They might say things like, "If you really cared about me, you wouldn't question what I say," or "Look at what you made me do." This tactic is especially disorienting because it twists your natural empathy into a weapon against you, leading you to prioritize the gaslighter's needs and emotions over your own well-being. It manipulates you into believing that you are the cause of their unhappiness or anger, shifting the blame from their actions to your supposed failures.

Along the same line, gaslighters often employ **projection and blame shifting**, accusing you of the very behaviors they are exhibiting and redirecting the responsibility for their actions onto you. For example, they might make a mistake or engage in poor behavior, but instead of owning up to it, they accuse you of being the catalyst. "You're the one who's making a big deal out of nothing" or "You're remembering it wrong" are common phrases that deny their accountability and challenge your perception and memory. It's a defense mechanism that throws you off balance and makes you defend yourself against accusations that have no basis, further distracting you from the gaslighter's behavior.

Psychological Effects of Gaslighting

This psychological manipulation extends to more than just mental confusion; it reaches into the realm of emotional abuse, where the abuser sows seeds of doubt about your competence, your emotional stability, and your worth. The impact? You might find yourself constantly on edge, hyper-aware of your every action and word, afraid of making mistakes, or worse, beginning to believe these negative portrayals.

Understanding these tactics is crucial. Recognizing when and how your reality is being questioned or altered can help you hold onto your truth. It empowers you to trust your instincts again, to rebuild that inner confidence that says, "I know what I experienced. I trust my perception."

This exploration of gaslighting isn't just about identifying tactics; it's about reclaiming your reality and affirming that no one has the right to manipulate your perception of the world. It's a crucial step in healing and taking back control of your life, ensuring you are no longer a puppet in someone else's play of power.

Counteracting Manipulation

One powerful way to begin this journey is to **trust your instincts**. Often, those gut feelings are your first signal that something isn't right. Even if your emotions have been consistently dismissed or mocked, remember that your feelings are valid and deserve attention. Start by acknowledging these feelings. Write them down if you need to. When you feel that twinge of doubt or discomfort, take a moment to explore it rather than push it aside. Trusting your instincts is like flexing a muscle—the more you listen to and validate them, the stronger and clearer they become.

Verifying your experiences is another essential strategy. This can be done by keeping a journal of events and conversations. When you write down what happened and how you felt about it, you create a personal record that can't be twisted by someone else's narrative. This record becomes a touchstone for your reality. Review it when you feel confused or unsure about what really occurred. It can help you see patterns of behavior that you might have missed and affirm your experiences and feelings.

Seeking external validation can also be immensely helpful. Doing this involves talking to trusted friends or a therapist who can provide perspective on your experiences. Sometimes, just voicing your concerns and hearing someone else acknowledge them can reinforce your understanding of reality. Choose someone who isn't connected to the gaslighter, if possible, to ensure an unbiased viewpoint. Remember, this journey is about restoring your autonomy and celebrating the resilience of your spirit.

THE PSYCHOLOGICAL IMPACT: FROM DOUBT TO DISORIENTATION

We started to talk about the psychological effects of gaslighting and manipulation, but there are deeper ways the manipulation of a narcissist could affect you. The constant push and pull of being adored one moment and devalued the next creates a whirlwind of confusion—a prime example of cognitive dissonance in action.

Cognitive Dissonance

Cognitive dissonance occurs when our beliefs and the information we are presented with—or the behaviors we are compelled to engage in—don't align, causing significant mental and emotional discomfort. In relationships dominated by a narcissist, you might find yourself justifying behaviors that deeply conflict with your values or rationalizing statements that you know, deep down, are false. For example, you might tell yourself, "They didn't mean it like that," or "They're just under a lot of stress," even when every fiber of your being screams that the treatment you're receiving is neither normal nor acceptable.

This dissonance can lead you to doubt your judgments and suppress your feelings to maintain peace or hold onto the relationship. It's a troubling cycle where the need to resolve these mental conflicts might compel you to alter your perceptions or memories of events to make them less painful or conflicting. The tragic irony here is that the very intelligence and empathy that allow you to see multiple sides of issues are what the narcissist manipulates to sow self-doubt (Arabi, 2024).

Erosion of Trust

Perhaps one of the most profound damages inflicted by narcissistic abuse is the erosion of trust. When you're constantly second-guessing your reality because someone close to you insists your memories are wrong or your feelings are misplaced, trust becomes a casualty in the battle for your sanity. Over time, this relentless undermining can significantly warp your ability to trust your own decisions and feelings. It feels as if you're walking through a maze blindfolded, unsure of which turn to take because the guidance you once relied on is now tainted by deception.

This erosion of trust doesn't limit itself to self-doubt; it spills over into other relationships. You may find yourself questioning the motives of friends who offer advice or support, worried that their intentions might not be genuine. The thought, "Can I really trust them, or will they betray me, too?" might loop through your mind, a residual effect of the manipulative tactics you've endured. This breakdown in trust creates a loneliness that is both profound and paralyzing, pushing you further into isolation.

Imagine trying to build or maintain relationships when you can't trust your judgment or believe in the reliability of your own emotions. The constant second-guessing of every interaction adds layers of unnecessary complexity, making straightforward relationships seem fraught with hidden meanings and potential threats.

Anxiety and Fear

The anxiety and fear that accompany this erosion of trust also cause profound psychological effects. They keep you in a state of heightened awareness, always on the lookout for the next blow, whether real or imagined. It's exhausting, disorienting, and deeply unsettling, leaving you yearning for solid ground that seems perpetually out of reach.

Living under constant criticism from a narcissist breeds a relentless fear of making mistakes. Every word you speak and every action you take feels like walking on eggshells, terrified that one wrong step could trigger an avalanche of blame, ridicule, or worse. It's not just about fearing their anger or disapproval but dreading how their reaction will make you feel—small, vulnerable, and more alone than ever.

The narcissist's criticism isn't limited to overt put-downs. It comes in subtle forms, too—backhanded compliments, undermining remarks, and expressions of disappointment that leave you questioning your worth. Over time, this constant drip of negativity erodes your confidence, convincing you that no matter what you do, you will always fall short.

Even simple decisions become fraught with anxiety. What should I wear today? Will this meal be good enough? Should I speak up or stay silent? Choices that once seemed straightforward now carry the weight of potential error and the dread of being met with contempt or disdain.

The ever-present criticism makes you hesitant, second-guessing your abilities and instincts. You might find yourself avoiding situations where your competence could be called into question, retreating into a shell where it feels safer to hide than to risk making a mistake. The desire to avoid criticism becomes a prison, limiting your world and leaving you perpetually anxious.

This anxiety, combined with the fear of not measuring up, can spill into other areas of your life. Relationships with friends and colleagues might become strained because you're constantly seeking reassurance or fearing their judgment. Tasks at work that once seemed routine now feel like daunting challenges. Every setback or misstep is magnified, feeding a cycle of self-doubt that keeps you locked in fear.

It's like living under a microscope, where every flaw is amplified, and every move is scrutinized. The fear isn't just of being criticized; it's the shame that comes with feeling like you'll never be good enough. It's a fear that makes you question your every action, word, and thought, leaving you paralyzed by the idea that no matter how hard you try, you will never escape the shadow of criticism.

Rebuilding Mental Stability

Rebuilding mental stability and regaining confidence in your perceptions and judgments is a journey that unfolds one step at a time. It's about reconnecting with your inner self, trusting in your own truth, and gradually dismantling the walls of doubt built by years of manipulation. While we've touched on trusting your intuition, journaling, and seeking external validation, other transformative strategies can further aid this healing process.

One effective way is through the practice of **mindfulness**. Mindfulness involves staying present and fully engaging with the now without judgment. You can anchor yourself in the present moment by focusing on your breath, the sensations in your body, or the sounds around you. This practice helps quiet the noise of past criticisms and future anxieties, allowing you to reconnect with your inner calm and clarity. Over time, mindfulness strengthens your ability to observe thoughts and feelings without immediately accepting them as truth, giving you space to evaluate them more objectively.

Another powerful tool is **affirmations**. Affirmations are positive, empowering statements that you can repeat to yourself to foster self-belief and counteract the negative, undermining messages you've internalized. Start with affirmations like, "I trust my judgment" or "My perceptions are accurate." These phrases, when repeated often, can begin to overwrite the negative narratives imposed by the narcissist, reinforcing your self-esteem and your trust in your own insights.

Engaging in **cognitive-behavioral strategies** can also be incredibly beneficial. This involves identifying specific negative thought patterns—such as overgeneralizing or catastrophizing—that may have been exacerbated by your experiences. By challenging these patterns and replacing them with more balanced and constructive thoughts, you can regain a more realistic perspective of yourself and your environment. For instance, instead of thinking, "I always make the wrong decisions because I've been told so," you might reframe it to, "I have made good decisions before, and I can learn from past mistakes to make better ones."

Reconnecting with your passions and interests can play a crucial role in rebuilding your mental stability. Engaging in activities that bring you joy and fulfillment can restore your sense of normalcy and boost your confidence. Whether it's art, nature, sports, or any other hobby, immersing yourself in what you love can remind you of your worth and your abilities, independent of anyone else's validation.

Together, these steps form a path back to a life where you feel secure in your thoughts and confident in your decisions. Remember, each step forward is a step away from the shadows of doubt and into the light of self-assuredness. We will explore each of these strategies in greater depth throughout this book, providing you with a comprehensive toolkit to reclaim your mental autonomy and rebuild your life on a foundation of self-trust and empowerment.

PHYSICAL SYMPTOMS OF EMOTIONAL ABUSE

The impact of emotional abuse extends far beyond the psychological realm, manifesting physically in ways that can both surprise and debilitate. When we are subjected to constant emotional turbulence, our bodies react as if facing a physical threat.

Stress Manifestations and Chronic Health Issues

Our brain, unable to distinguish between an attacking predator and psychological stress, triggers a flood of stress hormones like adrenaline and cortisol to prepare our bodies for fight or flight. This cascade of hormones increases our heart rate, raises our blood pressure, and boosts our energy temporarily, which might be beneficial if we were actually in physical danger. However, in the context of ongoing emotional abuse, where the threat is not physical, this response does not provide the relief or resolution that physical action might. Instead, it builds up, creating a state of chronic stress.

Under such conditions, cortisol, the primary stress hormone, disrupts the functions of non-essential systems for survival. It suppresses the digestive and reproductive systems and hampers immune responses. This can lead to a range of physical issues, including digestive problems like irritable bowel syndrome and chronic stomach inflammation, decreased fertility, and frequent infections. Elevated cortisol also disrupts normal metabolic and tissue repair processes, potentially causing weight gain and slowing bodily repair.

This hormonal imbalance exacerbates the psychological toll of constant criticism and manipulation, putting your body in a perpetual state of crisis preparedness. Over time, this can strain the cardiovascular system, as persistently high blood pressure and heart rate increase the risk of hypertension, heart attacks, and strokes. Muscular tension might also develop, leading to chronic pain and headaches.

Furthermore, the anxiety and depression commonly associated with long-term abuse can disrupt eating patterns, leading to under-eating or overeating, both of which adversely affect physical health. Chronic stress also often results in sleep disturbances; the inability to relax and ongoing worry can impair both the ability to fall and stay asleep, leading to sleep deprivation. This affects cognitive functions, complicates stress management, and generally degrades health (Mayo Clinic Staff, 2023).

Over time, prolonged exposure to high cortisol levels can disrupt almost all bodily processes, leading to chronic inflammation linked to numerous health issues, including heart disease, diabetes, and arthritis. The cumulative effect of these conditions places a significant burden on the body, showing the profound impact emotional abuse can have on physical health.

Healing the Body

Understanding how to react to stress in healthy ways is crucial. When you're under stress, it's easy to fall into habits that might feel comforting in the moment but can actually exacerbate your stress levels and physical health in the long run.

One foundational step is to cultivate a routine centered around **good nutrition and regular exercise**. Eating well helps stabilize your mood and energy levels, while physical activity is known to significantly decrease stress hormones like cortisol and adrenaline. It also stimulates the production of endorphins, the body's natural painkillers and mood elevators.

Ensuring you get **plenty of sleep** is another crucial element. Sleep has a profound impact on both mental and physical health, helping to repair the body, consolidate memory, and regulate emotions. Inadequate sleep can amplify the body's stress response and contribute to a vicious cycle of stress and sleeplessness.

Relaxation techniques such as yoga, meditation, and deep breathing exercises can also be incredibly effective. These practices help calm the mind and reduce the physical effects of stress on the body. Incorporating regular massages can further help reduce muscle tension and induce relaxation, offering a break from the chronic alertness driven by stress.

Fostering healthy relationships is equally important. Connecting with friends and family can provide incredible emotional support and reduce feelings of isolation, which are often exacerbated by stress. Having a sense of humor and finding reasons to laugh can also lighten your mental load and brighten your outlook on life.

If the stress becomes overwhelming, seeking professional counseling can be a wise step. A counselor can offer specific coping skills and strategies tailored to your needs, helping you manage stress more effectively.

Mind–Body Connection

While we focus on these practical steps, we cannot overlook the broader implications: the mind–body connection. Understanding how emotional healing can promote physical health is vital in this journey of recovery. When our emotional well-being is nurtured, it sets the stage for our physical systems to operate more effectively and harmoniously.

Emotional healing begins with addressing and processing the psychological traumas and stresses that may have accumulated over time. This process often involves therapies or activities that help us work through unresolved feelings, such as grief, fear, or anger. As we resolve these emotions, we often see a reduction in the physical symptoms associated with chronic stress, such as headaches, digestive issues, and sleep disturbances.

When you start to heal emotionally, it's like taking a heavy weight off your body. Stress hormones decrease, inflammation lowers, and your immune system begins to strengthen once again. This improvement comes because your body is no longer in a constant state of alert, no longer preparing to fight or flee. Instead, it can focus on restorative processes like healing and growth.

Moreover, emotional healing often leads to better habits and choices. With a clearer mind and a lighter heart, you're more likely to choose activities and foods that nourish rather than deplete you. You might find it easier to stick to a regular exercise routine or to choose restful sleep over late-night screen time. These choices, seemingly small day by day, accumulate into significant health improvements over time.

The beauty of focusing on emotional healing is that it doesn't just address symptoms; it works on the root causes of physical distress. By healing emotionally, you're not just patching up health issues as they arise—you're rebuilding the foundation of your overall health.

MOTHERHOOD UNDERMINED: THE EFFECTS ON PARENTING CONFIDENCE

Navigating motherhood is challenging under the best circumstances, but when you add the weight of narcissistic abuse, the impact on your confidence and decision-making as a mother can feel profound and disheartening. The constant manipulation and criticism from a narcissistic partner don't just affect how you view yourself; they can significantly alter how you approach parenting.

Impact on Parenting Style

When you're dealing with a narcissist, their needs and desires often take precedence, overshadowing your instincts and opinions. This dynamic can leave you second-guessing your choices as a mother. For instance, if you've ever felt confident about a parenting decision but then faced ridicule or dismissive remarks from a narcissistic partner, you might start to question your judgment. Over time, this can erode your confidence, making you feel less capable and more dependent on the narcissist's approval for validation.

This erosion of self-assurance seeps into the everyday aspects of parenting. You might hesitate to set boundaries for your children or struggle to advocate for their needs in school or social settings because you've been conditioned to doubt your capability to make good choices. The fear of criticism can make you overly cautious or indecisive, worrying that any misstep could lead to further conflict or disparagement.

Moreover, the unpredictability of a narcissistic partner's reactions can make the home environment tense and unstable. Trying to shield your children from this volatility while managing your own emotional turmoil takes a significant toll. It's challenging to feel like a competent, strong parent when you're constantly on edge, anticipating the next issue or navigating the fallout from the last confrontation.

This atmosphere can deeply influence how you interact with your children. You might find yourself either overly permissive to avoid conflict or too strict as you try to maintain some semblance of control in a chaotic environment. Neither approach feels genuinely aligned with your parenting values, but they might seem the only options when you're trying to keep the peace or assert some authority amid the confusion.

Living under the shadow of narcissistic abuse, the simple joy and connection that should be part of motherhood can become overshadowed by anxiety and doubt. The ongoing struggle to reclaim your sense of self in the face of such abuse is about improving your individual well-being and restoring the confidence you need to be the mother you want to be.

Protecting Your Children

Shielding your children from the negative impacts of witnessing abuse involves thoughtful strategies that prioritize their emotional safety and stability. First and foremost, it's vital to **foster open communication with your children**. This means creating a safe space where they feel they can express their feelings and concerns without fear of judgment or repercussions. Regular check-ins can help them feel supported and understood, and it also gives you a chance to gauge how they are coping with the environment at home.

Another key strategy is to **maintain as much routine and normalcy as possible**. Children thrive on predictability, and establishing consistent routines for meals, homework, bedtime, and leisure activities can provide a sense of security amid the uncertainty that often accompanies an abusive situation. These routines shouldn't just be rigid schedules; they should also include quality time together, such as reading stories, playing games, or going for walks, which can strengthen your bond and provide much-needed comfort and reassurance.

Additionally, it's crucial to **teach your children about healthy relationships and emotional intelligence**. This can involve discussions about what respectful behavior looks like, how to set personal boundaries, and the importance of kindness and empathy. These lessons can help them understand that the abusive behaviors they might witness are not normal or acceptable, equipping them with the knowledge to avoid similar dynamics in their own future relationships.

Creating a Supportive Environment

Creating a supportive environment and building a nurturing home for emotional and psychological growth involves both physical and emotional considerations. Physically, aim to make your home a place of comfort and peace. This can be as simple as setting up cozy spaces for relaxation, ensuring there are areas for play and creativity, and keeping the home organized and free from clutter. A calming, orderly space can significantly reduce stress and promote well-being.

Emotionally, it's about cultivating a positive atmosphere where love, respect, and support are at the forefront. Celebrate successes, no matter how small, and provide plenty of encouragement and positive reinforcement. This positive environment helps to counterbalance any negativity they might experience and fosters resilience.

It's also beneficial to involve your children in activities outside the home that can help build their confidence and sense of identity, such as sports, arts, or community service. Engaging with peers and mentors in these settings can further reinforce healthy social interactions and provide a break from any stress at home.

Through these actions, you're not just shielding your children; you're actively contributing to their emotional and psychological growth, helping them to develop into confident, well-adjusted individuals despite the challenges they might face at home. This nurturing approach protects and empowers them, providing a solid foundation for their future.

Rebuilding Confidence

Restoring your belief in your parenting abilities is a crucial step in overcoming the effects of narcissistic abuse. It starts with giving yourself permission to believe that you are a good parent, even if mistakes are made along the way. Recognizing that perfection is not the goal is fundamental—love, understanding, and growth are.

One effective action is to engage in **positive self-talk**. Instead of focusing on what you feel you've done wrong, remind yourself of what you've done right. Celebrate the moments when you made your child laugh, provided comfort, or navigated a difficult situation successfully. Acknowledging these successes, no matter how small, can rebuild your confidence and reinforce your identity as a capable, caring parent.

Another powerful step is to **seek feedback from trustworthy sources**. This could be friends, family, or even your children themselves. Ask them what they think you do well as a parent. Often, their responses can highlight strengths you may have overlooked or undervalued, providing a much-needed boost to your self-esteem.

Educating yourself on parenting techniques can also be incredibly empowering. Whether through books, workshops, or credible online resources, gaining knowledge about child development, effective communication, and healthy discipline strategies can make you feel more prepared and competent. This education benefits your parenting approach and reinforces your ability to make informed decisions for your family's well-being.

Additionally, **consider joining support groups or online communities of parents**. Sharing experiences and challenges can help you see that you're not alone in your struggles. These groups provide a platform for encouragement and advice and can be a reminder that everyone is learning and growing in their parental role. Witnessing others in similar situations striving to improve can be incredibly motivating and affirming.

It is important to allow yourself time to reflect on your parenting journey. Look back at where you started and where you are now. Recognize the growth, not just in your children, but in yourself as a parent. Understanding that growth is a process and seeing tangible evidence of your progress can significantly restore your belief in your abilities.

FINANCIAL AND SOCIAL ISOLATION: REBUILDING YOUR SUPPORT SYSTEM

Narcissists often use isolation as a tool to increase control over their victims, and this can manifest in particularly damaging ways when it comes to severing financial resources and social networks. By cutting you off from these vital supports, a narcissist ensures that you become more dependent on them, thus solidifying their power in the relationship.

Recognizing Isolation Tactics

Financial isolation typically begins subtly. It might start with suggestions or criticisms about your spending habits or your ability to manage money effectively. Gradually, these comments can escalate into demands to oversee your financial accounts or relinquish your control over them. You might find yourself having to justify every purchase or, in more severe cases, asking for an allowance. This control over your financial resources limits your independence, making it incredibly difficult to make decisions or leave the relationship without facing significant financial hardship.

Social isolation follows a similar, insidious path. Initially, a narcissist might monopolize your time or subtly criticize your friends and family, planting seeds of doubt about their intentions or their liking for you. These tactics can escalate to outright demands to cut ties or to spend less time with others, often justified by professing love or the need to prioritize the relationship above all else. Before you know it, you may find your social circle has dwindled, leaving you feeling alone and unsupported—exactly as the narcissist intends.

By undermining your relationships with others, a narcissist effectively removes critical sources of support and differing perspectives. This isolation makes it harder for you to maintain a sense of reality outside of the narcissist's influence and ensures that you have fewer opportunities to voice your experiences or get help. The lack of a support network can make you feel that there is no way out and no one to turn to, deepening the emotional and psychological hold the narcissist has on you.

These strategies are particularly destructive because they attack the very foundations of your autonomy and resilience, making it a challenge to stand up to the abuser or to make choices that could help you regain your independence. Understanding these tactics is the first step in recognizing the mechanisms of control in such relationships.

Rebuilding Financial Independence

Rebuilding financial independence and regaining control over your financial life after experiencing isolation in an abusive relationship involves several critical steps. This process is empowering and crucial for establishing a secure foundation for your future.

The first step toward financial autonomy is **understanding your current financial status**. Start by reviewing all your accounts and financial holdings. Knowing exactly what resources you have at your disposal provides a clear starting point. From there, set up a budget that accounts for your income and expenses. This helps in making informed decisions about your spending and saving, ensuring that you are living within your means and planning for future needs.

Updating your financial information is also essential. If you've undergone a name change or changed your address post-separation, ensure all your financial documents and accounts reflect this. This includes your bank accounts, credit cards, driver's license, and any other legal documents. Also, if any financial assets need to be transferred or updated, such as titles on cars or deeds to property, take care of these changes promptly.

Building your credit is another vital step. Start by obtaining a copy of your credit report to understand where you stand and address any inaccuracies. If you're starting from scratch or have a thin credit file, consider applying for a secured credit card or becoming an authorized user on a trusted person's account to begin establishing credit. Regular, on-time payments and careful management of your credit limits will gradually improve your credit score, which is crucial for future financial independence.

Seeking the advice of a financial advisor can also be incredibly beneficial. Choose someone experienced in handling post-divorce financial planning, particularly if your separation involved complex financial settlements. A financial advisor can help you manage any lump sum payments from your divorce settlement, invest wisely, and plan for long-term goals like retirement or your children's education.

Finally, **establish a system for ongoing financial management**. This includes setting up direct deposits for your income, automating bill payments to avoid late fees, and regularly reviewing and adjusting your budget and financial plans as your circumstances change (Landers, 2012).

If you take these steps, you regain control over your financial situation and build a buffer against future uncertainties. As you grow more confident in managing your finances, you'll find that this confidence spills over into other areas of your life. Remember, financial independence is not just about money—it's about freedom, security, and the ability to make choices that are best for you and your children. Each step you take rebuilds the stable ground beneath your feet, allowing you to move forward with strength and assurance.

CREATING A SAFETY NET AND RECONNECTING SOCIALLY

Creating a safety net through a robust support system is an invaluable step toward recovery and resilience after enduring a relationship marked by narcissistic abuse. This support system offers both emotional and practical assistance, helping to buffer against the hardships of recovery and providing a solid base for rebuilding your life.

To start, focus on reconnecting with old friends and family members. Relationships may have been strained or neglected during the time of abuse, but reach out to these people, explaining your situation as much as you are comfortable. You'll find that many are willing to offer support and under-standing, and these rekindled relationships can provide immense comfort and a sense of normalcy.

In addition to re-establishing old ties, actively seek out new connections. Joining clubs, groups, or classes that align with your interests can be a great way to meet new people who share your passions. Whether it's a book club, a fitness class, or a crafting group, these social settings provide opportuni-ties to form new friendships in environments that are posi-tive and engaging.

Volunteering is another powerful way to expand your support network while also giving back to the community. It can boost your self-esteem, connect you with people who have similar values, and add a rewarding and meaningful activity to your life. Volunteering can also offer a new perspective on your own situation, which can be incredibly enlightening and healing.

Social media and online communities can also be valuable resources, especially if your physical mobility is limited or you're not quite ready for lots of in-person interaction. Many online groups are dedicated to supporting individuals who have gone through similar experiences. These platforms allow you to connect with others who can offer empathy, advice, and encouragement from the comfort of your home. This network can aid in healing and enrich your life, providing strength and companionship as you navigate the path forward.

THE SILENT SUFFERING: EMOTIONAL ABUSE BEHIND CLOSED DOORS

To wrap up this comprehensive chapter that lays the ground-work for our journey through narcissistic abuse recovery, let's now explore the hidden nature of emotional abuse. Understanding why this form of abuse is often difficult to recognize and identifying its signs are both crucial steps in protecting ourselves and aiding others who may be suffering in silence.

Emotional abuse is insidious. It doesn't generally leave physical marks, making it less apparent to outside observers and sometimes even the victims themselves. Instead, it chips away at a person's self-esteem, autonomy, and perception of reality through continuous manipulation, criticism, and intimidation.

One reason emotional abuse is so hard to recognize is that it often starts subtly. It might begin with slight criticisms or dismissive remarks that seem benign but gradually escalate to more overt and harmful behaviors. The abuser's actions may be framed as care or concern, confusing the victim and making it difficult to pinpoint the moment when the behavior became abusive. Over time, these behaviors become a constant, toxic presence in the victim's life, yet their gradual onset makes them easier to dismiss or rationalize.

Identifying the signs of emotional abuse is key to acknowledging its presence and beginning the process of recovery. Common signs include:

- **The feeling of walking on eggshells:** Constant anxiety about how to avoid provoking the abuser's anger or criticism.
- **Isolation:** Being cut off from family and friends, often at the abuser's insistence, under the guise of love or jealousy.
- **Degradation:** Frequent belittling or put-downs, often under the guise of "jokes" or "just being honest."
- **Control:** Excessive control over aspects of your life, such as how you dress, who you see, and where you go.
- **Withholding affection as punishment:** The abuser may refuse to communicate or show affection as a form of punishment and control.
- **Gaslighting:** As we discussed, this makes you doubt your own memory or perception of events, which leads you to question your sanity.

Breaking the Silence

Speaking out and seeking help after enduring narcissistic abuse is an act of bravery. It requires breaking through the fog of manipulation and finding your voice amidst the chaos of self-doubt. The courage it takes to reach out and share your story is monumental, and it can be the key to unlocking the path toward healing.

One of the first strategies for speaking out is to find someone you trust—a friend, family member, or therapist—who can listen without judgment. Sometimes, just having a supportive ear can lighten the burden and help you gain clarity. Choose someone who has shown empathy and understanding in the past and who you believe will respect your experiences.

If you feel uncomfortable sharing with someone in your immediate circle, consider reaching out to a support group, either locally or online. The power of shared experiences cannot be overstated. Finding others who have walked a similar path and are willing to listen and offer support can be incredibly validating. In these groups, you'll discover you're not alone and that the abuse wasn't your fault—a realization that can be transformative in overcoming the stigma of abuse.

When seeking help, it's also crucial to remember that professional assistance can be life changing. Therapists who specialize in trauma and abuse understand the nuances of emotional manipulation and can guide you through the healing process with compassion and expertise. Don't hesitate to reach out to a mental health professional or a local advocacy group specializing in domestic violence or emotional abuse. They can offer counseling, resources, and legal advice tailored to your situation.

Overcoming the stigma of abuse starts with acknowledging your own strength and courage. Remind yourself daily that speaking up is an act of empowerment, not shame. You are breaking free from the narrative imposed on you and reclaiming your right to live without fear or manipulation.

And remember, healing is not a linear journey. There will be ups and downs, moments of triumph, and moments of struggle. But with each step forward, whether through speaking out, seeking help, or finding solidarity in shared experiences, you are building a brighter, more resilient future. Trust in your strength, reach out for support, and know that your voice matters.

2

THE JOURNEY THROUGH GRIEF
AND ACCEPTANCE

> "*I will not say: do not weep; for not all tears are an evil.*"
>
> — J.R.R. TOLKIEN, THE RETURN OF THE KING

During one long, sleepless night, sitting quietly in the dim light of the living room while my daughters slept peacefully upstairs, my reality became painfully clear. Surrounded by the scattered remnants of my former life and the debris of a marriage I once thought was built on mutual love and respect, I felt the ground shift beneath me. I had been living in a carefully constructed illusion, a narrative spun by someone I trusted implicitly but who, in truth, had been manipulating every thread of our lives together.

This chapter is about walking through that painful realization and learning to accept the unvarnished truth of our experiences. It's about grieving for the relationship I thought I had and the part of myself that was lost in the deception.

Grieving is a complex journey, one that involves peeling back layers of pain and confronting the raw, sometimes brutal realities that emerge. It's also about the crucial stages of grief that come with narcissistic abuse, each stage a step on a path toward healing.

As we learn to let go of the past, we must find ways to release the attachments to the illusions we once held so dear. This process is never easy—there's a profound sense of betrayal that can shake the very foundation of your world. But there's also closure in acknowledging the truth, even if that closure doesn't include an apology or acknowledgment from those who wronged us.

Acceptance plays a huge role in this journey. It isn't about approving what happened or minimizing the pain—it's about accepting that the mistreatment was real and it impacted you deeply. This acceptance doesn't tie you to the past but frees you to rebuild a future unchained from those painful memories. It involves radical acceptance of the facts, shifting perspectives to empower yourself, and cultivating deep, forgiving compassion toward oneself.

Moreover, dealing with the intense emotions like denial, bargaining, and anger that often accompany this journey is crucial. Each emotion must be understood and processed constructively to avoid becoming trapped in an endless cycle that prevents true healing. Anger, when channeled correctly, can be a powerful catalyst for change, pushing you toward actions that reinforce your self-worth and propel you forward.

As we navigate through the depths of sadness and depression that can follow in the wake of such profound betrayal, we must also learn to reach out for help—embracing therapy, community support, and strategies that nurture our mental and physical well-being.

Ultimately, this chapter is about turning the page. It's about embracing acceptance that leads to personal growth and finding hope that lights the path ahead. It's about setting goals and envisioning a life beyond the shadows of abuse—a life where you, and only you, define your worth and your future. Let's walk this path together, step by step, toward a horizon filled with promise and newfound strength.

MOURNING THE ILLUSION: GRIEVING THE RELATIONSHIP YOU THOUGHT YOU HAD

Facing reality after living under the spell of a narcissist involves a profound and often painful awakening. For years, maybe even decades, the illusion crafted by a narcissist can feel as real as anything grounded in truth. This illusion—a fabricated blend of half-truths and outright fabrications—is designed to keep you tethered to the narcissist, dependent on their version of reality.

The process begins when you start noticing the discrepancies—small cracks in the facade that don't quite add up. Perhaps it's a pattern of behavior that contradicts their proclaimed devotion or promises that never manifest into reality. As these inconsistencies accumulate, a picture starts to emerge that is starkly different from the one painted by the narcissist.

This awakening is jarring. Realizing that the person you trusted most has been manipulating your reality can feel like a betrayal of the deepest kind. It shakes the foundations of what you believed was true about your life, your relationship, and even your own perceptions. It's not just discovering that you've been lied to; it's realizing that the emotional environment you've been living in has been carefully engineered to serve someone else's needs at the expense of your own.

Embracing this reality is crucial, though. It's the first step toward reclaiming your sense of self and beginning the healing process. This involves deconstructing the narrative you've been fed and recognizing the abuse for what it truly is. It's about distinguishing the romantic gestures that once seemed like signs of love from the manipulative tactics they actually were—designed to keep you loyal, compliant, and emotionally invested in the relationship.

STAGES OF GRIEF

As you peel away each layer of deception and confront the harsh truths beneath, you inevitably begin to mourn. You grieve not only for the relationship you thought you had but for the time lost to someone who never truly had your best interests at heart. This mourning is where we enter the stages of grief, navigating through a journey that is uniquely complex when it stems from narcissistic abuse.

The first stage, **denial**, serves as a defense mechanism that initially cushions the blow of reality. It's that fleeting comfort of thinking, "This isn't happening; they will change, or perhaps I'm just overreacting." Denial helps manage the overwhelming pain of betrayal, but eventually, as its veil lifts, the full impact of the truth begins to settle in.

Following closely is **anger**. This stage is visceral and can feel all-consuming. It's a reaction to the recognition of the time, energy, and emotion wasted on a facade. Anger in this context isn't just fury directed at the narcissist; it's also a profound upset directed at the universe for allowing such deceit, and sometimes, at oneself for being ensnared by it.

Bargaining often emerges from a place of vulnerability. It's filled with "what ifs" and "if only" statements that reflect a desperate attempt to regain control or revert to a time before the abuse. It's a painful clutch at the straws of a past that felt safer, where you might find yourself negotiating with reality, trying to find alternate endings to your pain.

Depression follows when the weight of what you have lost truly sinks in. It is more than sadness; it is an enveloping blanket of exhaustion and disinterest in life. The future might seem bleak, and detachment from joy can become the norm. It's in this stage that the isolation enforced by the narcissist can feel most potent, as the emotional resources to reach out or connect may feel utterly depleted.

Finally, **acceptance** doesn't imply happiness or resolution but rather an understanding of your reality. It's the stage where you acknowledge that the abuse occurred and recognize that it has shaped your experience, but it does not define your future. Acceptance involves a hard-won peace with the past and a slow movement toward healing (Holland, 2023).

It is here, in understanding and working through these stages, that we find tools for future resilience. Each stage, with its challenges and revelations, contributes to a deeper self-knowledge and a fortified spirit ready to rebuild from the ruins left by deception. It's with this knowledge and these experiences that we begin to truly heal, finding our way out of the shadows of grief.

The Role of Denial in Narcissistic Abuse Recovery

Before we can embrace acceptance, we navigate the first stage of grief, which is denial. This initial phase serves as a natural defense mechanism, helping to buffer the immediate shock of traumatic experiences. Denial can manifest subtly, as you might find yourself downplaying the abuse or rationalizing the narcissist's behavior. It's a way to shield yourself from the full brunt of the pain, at least temporarily.

In the context of narcissistic abuse, denial often serves another critical function—it preserves the vital but fragile thread of hope that things might return to the way they once seemed. You might catch yourself thinking, "It wasn't always this bad," or "Maybe they'll change back to the person I first fell in love with." These thoughts are reflections of wishful thinking and part of a deeply ingrained survival tactic that keeps the overwhelming reality of the situation at bay.

Denial also manifests in how you might minimize the abuse when speaking with friends or family or even to yourself. You may focus on the good days or make excuses for the narcissist's behavior, attributing it to stress, work, or just a bad moment. By doing so, you avoid confronting the painful truth and the significant changes that acknowledgment would demand.

However, living in denial can only offer protection for so long. The reality inevitably presses in, and the dam built by denial eventually begins to crack. This is when the suppressed emotions start to surface, and the pain that was held at bay comes flooding through. It's an overwhelming phase but a necessary transition as it pushes you toward facing the truths you've been avoiding.

Anger and Its Place in Healing: Channeling Your Rage Constructively

And then there's anger. This next stage emerges as a natural response to the recognition of lost time, shattered trust, and the emotional toll taken by living under the shadow of manipulation. Anger in this context is not only expected but entirely justified. It can surge as a potent, fiery force, reflecting the depth of betrayal felt upon confronting the reality of abuse. This emotion, while intense, is an integral part of the healing journey, signaling a break away from the denial that may have clouded your reality.

Anger becomes a catalyst that propels you forward. It can energize you to take action, to set boundaries, and to demand respect. It is a clarion call that often leads to reclaiming your sense of self that was suppressed by the narcissist's demeaning behaviors. Yet, the challenge lies not just in feeling anger but in channeling it constructively. When harnessed correctly, anger fuels the drive to advocate for yourself, seek support, and engage in self-care practices that fortify your emotional and psychological well-being.

Learning to channel your anger involves recognizing its sources and expressing it in healthy ways. Instead of letting anger turn into bitterness or vengefulness, you can use it to motivate changes in your life that enhance your independence and well-being. Activities like physical exercise, engaging in art, or writing can serve as outlets for these intense emotions, providing a means to expel negativity without causing further harm to yourself or others.

Therapeutic strategies such as cognitive-behavioral therapy (CBT) can also play a crucial role in anger management. They help you understand the triggers of your anger, dissect unhealthy thought patterns, and develop coping mechanisms that redirect this powerful emotion into actions that support healing and growth.

Recognizing and Moving Beyond Bargaining

The third stage is bargaining. At this juncture, you may find yourself caught in a cycle of conditional thinking, marked by a stream of "what ifs" and "if onlys." This stage represents an attempt to negotiate with the pain, a way to potentially undo the hurt or find a solution that can erase the past. You might catch yourself thinking, "If only I had recognized the signs earlier," or "What if I had done something differently?" These thoughts reflect a natural desire to regain control over a situation that once made you feel powerless.

Bargaining can also manifest as a negotiation with fate or a higher power, where you promise changes or actions in hopes of a different outcome, even though it's already too late. This mental bargaining is a defense mechanism that temporarily cushions the blow of reality, providing a temporary escape from painful truths.

However, while it's a natural part of the healing process, getting stuck in this stage can impede progress. In order to move beyond bargaining, it's important to confront and accept the reality that the past cannot be changed. An effective strategy is to redirect your focus toward things within your control—like your reaction to what happened.

Embracing this mindset, we can learn a lot from stoicism, an ancient philosophy that teaches us the value of focusing on what we can control and letting go of what we cannot. By concentrating on our responses and decisions, we become more resilient and empowered. Stoicism doesn't mean suppressing emotions or hardships; rather, it involves acknowledging our feelings as valid but choosing not to be overwhelmed by them.

In practice, this might mean when I face a setback, I try to view it as an opportunity for growth. Instead of asking, "Why is this happening to me?" I can ask, "What can I learn from this?" This shift in perspective helps me find peace and move forward. Remember, it's about doing what we can with what we have where we are. Each small step you take in managing your reactions helps you regain a sense of control and paves the way for healing and growth.

Depression: Navigating the Depth of Sadness

As you begin to release the hold that bargaining has on you, the path leads you toward deeper introspection and acceptance and into the next phase of your healing journey. We can expect the fourth stage, which is depression, where the emotional weight of what you have endured might feel more pronounced as you start to deal with the loss more directly.

Understanding the connection between abuse and depression is crucial as you navigate this stage. Narcissistic abuse, by its nature, is profoundly isolating and demeaning, often leading to significant psychological distress. It's not uncommon for survivors to experience intense feelings of worthlessness, hopelessness, and an overwhelming sense of loss—core components of depression. These feelings can stem from months or even years of being undermined, manipulated, and gaslighted, leaving you questioning your own worth and reality (Cuncic, 2023).

Recognizing the signs of depression in yourself is an essential part of the healing process. Symptoms might include persistent sadness, loss of interest in activities you once enjoyed, changes in appetite or weight, sleep disturbances, fatigue, feelings of guilt or worthlessness, difficulty concentrating, and thoughts of death or suicide. It's important to acknowledge these signs without judgment and understand that they are common responses to the trauma you've experienced.

Depression in the context of narcissistic abuse recovery can make you feel stuck, as if you're in a fog that won't lift. This stage of grief is less about the acute pain of anger or bargaining and more about coming to terms with the depth of what you've lost. It involves mourning not just the end of the relationship but the impact of the abuse on your self-esteem and outlook on life.

When navigating through this stage, it's helpful to seek support from mental health professionals who understand the nuances of narcissistic abuse. Therapy can provide a safe space to express and explore these heavy emotions. Additionally, joining support groups where you can connect with others who have faced similar situations can be incredibly validating and reassuring.

Engaging in self-care practices is also vital. Simple activities like maintaining a routine, eating nutritious meals, getting regular exercise, and ensuring enough sleep can make a significant difference in your mental health. These actions help stabilize your mood and improve your energy levels, making it easier to cope with the symptoms of depression.

Acceptance and Hope: The Art of Letting Go

To navigate out of the deep sadness and anxiety you might be enveloped in, you first need to embrace the reality of your experiences. Recognizing that depression is a response to what you've been through—and not a reflection of your worth or capabilities—is crucial. This acknowledgment is a pivotal step toward healing, setting the stage for eventual acceptance and the possibility of hope that lies beyond the current pain.

From this place of understanding, forgiving yourself becomes a key aspect of recovery. It's essential to let go of the self-blame that so often accompanies the aftermath of narcissistic abuse. Remember, the manipulation you experienced was designed to skew your perceptions and control your reactions. Overcoming this means actively working to dismantle the false beliefs instilled by the abuser and reaffirming your own reality and worth.

Forgiveness is not about excusing the narcissist's behavior, nor is it about forgetting the pain caused. Instead, it's about freeing yourself from the burden of ongoing resentment and bitterness. Start by challenging the critical inner voices that echo the narcissist's words. Replace them with affirmations of your strengths, your resilience, and your right to happiness.

Practical steps for finding closure are also important, especially without expecting acknowledgment or apology from the abuser. Closure comes from within. It means making peace with the fact that the person who hurt you may never fully understand or atone for the damage they've caused. This can be achieved through therapeutic practices like writing a letter to the abuser that you never send, which can articulate your feelings and assert your truth without the vulnerability of direct confrontation.

Letting go of the past and releasing attachments to the illusion requires you to stay grounded in the present. Mindfulness practices can be incredibly beneficial here. Activities like meditation, yoga, or even simple breathing exercises can help anchor you in the now, enabling you to appreciate your life as it is, free from the distortions imposed by someone else.

ACCEPTING THE UNACCEPTABLE: FINDING PEACE WITH THE PAST

Better than just accepting, we can radically accept. **Radical acceptance** is about embracing the reality and truth of what happened, fully acknowledging the events and their impact without resistance or denial. It's a foundation for healing because it allows us to move forward, unburdened by the weight of "what ifs" and "could have beens."

Radical acceptance means facing the hard truth that the person you loved, who you believed was your partner, was, in fact, someone else entirely. It's letting go of the illusion that they will change or that things could have been different if only you'd done something differently. It's understanding that no amount of wishing or bargaining will alter the past and that the abuse you endured was never your fault.

This process is not about condoning what happened or minimizing the pain. Instead, it's about freeing yourself from the mental trap of hoping for a reality that will never come to pass. It's about recognizing that the relationship wasn't what you thought it was and that the promises and dreams were never grounded in truth.

Embracing this truth isn't easy, and it can be incredibly painful at first. It involves facing the betrayal and manipulation head-on, acknowledging how deeply it hurt, and accepting the scars it left behind. But this acceptance becomes the cornerstone of your healing journey because it allows you to stop expending emotional energy on something that can no longer be changed.

In radically accepting the past, you also begin to radically accept yourself. You let go of the guilt and self-blame that the narcissist may have planted in your mind. You stop berating yourself for staying too long or not seeing the signs earlier. Instead, you recognize that you did your best with the information you had at the time and that you deserve compassion for the pain you've endured.

Moving forward with this newfound acceptance, you create space for growth and self-compassion. You lay a foundation for building a life based on truth and self-respect, where you are free to make decisions that serve your well-being without being chained to the wounds of the past.

Radical acceptance doesn't happen overnight. It's a daily practice of reminding yourself that the past cannot be changed, but your future is still within your control. And with each moment of acceptance, you strengthen your resolve, empowering yourself to move forward with clarity and courage.

ENVISIONING A BRIGHTER FUTURE

Ultimately, radical acceptance is about building a new foundation for yourself, one that is based on reality, self-compassion, and personal strength. By laying this groundwork, you pave the way to a future unchained from the past, where acceptance is not seen as defeat but as empowerment. This journey will then lead you to build a new foundation, lay the groundwork for a future unchained from the past, and view acceptance not as defeat but as empowerment, marking a pivotal transformation in reclaiming your life and your autonomy.

As you step into this new phase of your life, it's essential to start setting tangible goals that align with the vision of the life you desire beyond the shadow of abuse. Think about what a life filled with joy, fulfillment, and peace looks like for you. Maybe it includes pursuing a new career, dedicating time to hobbies that were pushed aside, or simply cultivating a daily routine that nourishes your soul.

Start by identifying small, achievable goals that lead to bigger aspirations. Perhaps it's enrolling in a class that interests you, joining a community group, or planning regular meet-ups with friends. Each goal should act as a stepping-stone that builds your confidence and reinforces your independence.

Imagining your life beyond abuse also involves a crucial shift in mindset—from seeing yourself as a victim to viewing yourself as a survivor and a creator of your destiny. This mindset shift is empowering and catalyzes a deep internal transformation that affects all aspects of your life.

The first steps toward rebuilding your life on your terms involve concrete actions like redecorating your living space to reflect your tastes, establishing new traditions that celebrate your freedom, and setting boundaries that protect your emotional and physical well-being. It's about making daily choices that affirm your values and your right to live freely and fully.

As we prepare to explore the next chapter, we'll explore deeper into how you can reclaim your self-identity and self-worth. We will discuss the importance of celebrating your individuality, setting healthy boundaries, rediscovering your passions, and connecting with those who uplift and support you. Each step is crucial in creating a vibrant life marked by resilience and renewal.

This journey is not just about recovery; it's about thriving. It's about reclaiming every piece of your individuality that was overshadowed by someone else's needs. So, join me as we take these steps together, embracing the life you deserve with open arms.

3

RECLAIMING SELF-IDENTITY AND SELF-WORTH

66 *"I am, I can, I will, I do."*

— *CHRISTINE D'ERCOLE*

One moment, I stood in front of the mirror, staring at a reflection I barely recognized. The face looking back at me seemed like a distant version of myself, one that had been muted and reshaped by years under someone else's shadow. It was a profound wake-up call when I realized just how much of myself I had lost to my marriage—my interests, my dreams, and even my laughter had become casualties of the oppressive environment I had been living in.

This realization marked the beginning of a significant journey for me—a journey to reclaim the person I was before the tumultuousness and to discover who I am now in its aftermath. It's about peeling back the layers of who I was told to be and finding the authentic self that had been buried underneath.

The path to rediscovering oneself after severing ties with a toxic partner is both challenging and exhilarating. It involves mourning the loss of the person you might have been if circumstances were different while simultaneously celebrating the emergence of who you can become. This process is not just about healing; it's about rebuilding a self that is all the stronger for what it has endured.

In reclaiming your identity, you begin a journey of self-discovery that encourages you to explore personal interests, values, and goals that were suppressed or set aside. It's about constructing a new self-concept that aligns with your true self, not the distorted image reflected by someone else's needs.

Celebrating your individuality becomes a crucial part of this process. It's about recognizing and embracing your unique qualities and strengths and understanding that these attributes are worth celebrating. Every small step in this journey is a step away from the shadows of abuse and into the light of self-acceptance.

As we move forward, you'll learn how shifting from seeing yourself as a victim to viewing yourself as a survivor and thriver can transform your life. We'll explore how setting boundaries is not just an act of self-care but a profound act of self-respect. We'll also rediscover the joy and passion of old and new interests, viewing these pursuits not just as hobbies but as vital acts of resistance against the abuse endured.

This process is more than a recovery; it's a renaissance of the self, an opportunity to mold your identity with intention and grace. Let's embrace this journey together with open hearts and an unwavering commitment to our newfound autonomy. This will then lead you to build a new foundation, lay the groundwork for a future unchained from the past, and view acceptance as empowerment, marking a pivotal transformation in reclaiming your life and your autonomy.

THE MIRROR'S NEW REFLECTION: RECLAIMING YOUR IDENTITY POST-ABUSE

Narcissistic abuse often starts with a whirlwind of charm and love bombing, but as the relationship progresses, the idealization phase gives way to a stark and devastating reality. The devaluation phase of narcissistic abuse is where the most significant distortion of self-image begins. In this phase, the abuser's demeanor shifts dramatically—from adoration to contempt—plunging the victim into an abyss of emotional turmoil and confusion (Wakefield, 2023).

During this period, the abuser systematically dismantles the victim's self-esteem. They belittle achievements, criticize every action, and inflict deep psychological wounds. The once-celebrated qualities of the victim are now points of relentless criticism. This constant negativity serves as a powerful tool in eroding the victim's identity, making them question their worth and reality. Insults, gaslighting, and perpetual put-downs are wielded not just to control but to fundamentally alter how the victim perceives themselves.

The intermittent reinforcement that follows—cycles of punishment interspersed with moments of kindness—creates trauma bonds. These bonds tie the victim to the abuser, making it difficult to leave despite the abuse. This phase leaves the victim in a state of anxiety and distress, walking on eggshells, ever fearful of inciting the abuser's wrath and desperately trying to regain the affection once freely given.

In this environment, the victim's self-image is often completely dismantled. They may begin to see themselves through the distorted lens provided by the abuser: incompetent, unworthy, and unlovable. This skewed self-perception can have profound implications, affecting not only the victim's relationship with the abuser but also their relationships with others and their sense of self outside of any relationship.

As the abuser projects their idealized self-image onto the victim, demanding they live up to an impossible standard, the victim's identity becomes increasingly tied to the whims and criticisms of their abuser. The message is clear: You are not enough unless you reflect what I want you to be. This can leave victims feeling lost and unsure of who they are without the validation they've become conditioned to seek from their abuser.

Recognizing this distortion is the first crucial step in reclaiming your self-image. The path to recovery involves acknowledging the abuse and its impacts and understanding that the erosion of your identity was a result of manipulation, not a reflection of your true self.

Self-Discovery Journey: Building a New Self-Concept

That's when we begin a self-discovery journey. This journey is about peeling back the layers of influence and control to build a new self-concept and uncover the authentic person underneath. It's about redefining who you are on your terms, not through the warped perspective of someone else's needs and insecurities. This process is both liberating and essential, a path to healing that restores the self-worth and independence that narcissistic abuse seeks to destroy.

Constructing this new self involves several crucial steps. First, engage in **deep introspection**. Ask yourself what truly matters to you, what you value, and what brings you joy. This might mean reconnecting with old passions or discovering new interests that ignite excitement and enthusiasm. It's about listening to your inner voice, the one that might have been silenced or ignored during times of manipulation.

Second, **set clear goals that align with your true self**. These goals should be guided by what you've discovered during your introspection. They might be related to personal development, such as pursuing education or career aspirations that were previously put on hold. They might also be about personal well-being, like improving physical health, emotional resilience, or spiritual growth.

Third, **practice self-compassion**. Understand that healing is a process, and it's okay to have moments of doubt or weakness. Be kind to yourself and recognize that each step forward, no matter how small, is progress. Affirmations can be a powerful tool here. Regularly affirming your worth, your strengths, and your right to happiness can help solidify your evolving self-concept.

As you work through these steps, you'll find that you are building a solid foundation for your new self—one that is robust, defined by your own standards, and resilient in the face of future challenges. This new self is not a fixed state but a continuous evolution, adapting and growing through all of life's experiences.

CELEBRATING INDIVIDUALITY

Celebrating your individuality then becomes a pivotal strategy in this journey. Embracing what makes you unique is not just about acknowledging your attributes—it's about actively showcasing them and integrating them into your daily life. This celebration is a bold declaration of your independence and a reaffirmation of your worth, especially after a period where your identity might have been overshadowed or suppressed.

To truly celebrate your individuality, start by **reflecting on the qualities and strengths that define you**. What are the characteristics that others admire in you? What skills or talents do you possess that make you feel proud? These can range from interpersonal skills like empathy and compassion to creative abilities or intellectual pursuits. Write these down, and revisit this list often, especially on days when you feel unsure of your path.

Next, **find ways to express these qualities in your life**. If creativity is a significant part of who you are, engage in creative activities regularly, whether that's painting, writing, or crafting. If you're a natural leader, seek opportunities to lead, whether in your community, workplace, or social groups. Expressing these traits can reinforce your self-worth and remind you of your value as an individual.

Also, **surround yourself with people who recognize and celebrate your unique qualities**. Positive reinforcement from friends, family, and peers can bolster your self-esteem and help cement your sense of identity. This network of support not only affirms your individuality but also provides a mirror that reflects your true self back to you, free from the distortions of past abuse.

Sharing your journey and your victories, big or small, with others can also be a powerful way to celebrate your individuality. Whether through social media, blogging, or simply conversations with friends, speaking openly about your experiences and growth can inspire others and further affirm your personal development.

FROM VICTIM TO SURVIVOR: SHIFTING YOUR SELF-PERCEPTION

It's also crucial to challenge the narratives that once confined you. You must move beyond the victim label to see yourself as the protagonist in your life story. This shift in perspective isn't about denying the pain you've experienced but about reframing it as part of a larger narrative of survival and empowerment. By doing so, you transform your identity from one defined by what happened to you to one shaped by how you've overcome hardships.

Redefining your identity this way involves acknowledging your past and the lessons it taught you while not allowing it to dictate your present or future. It means looking at the adversities you faced not just as sources of pain but also as opportunities that contributed to your growth and strength. Every challenge you've navigated has equipped you with unique insights and resilience, qualities that define a survivor.

To adopt this empowered identity, start by **recognizing and celebrating your victories**, no matter how small. Each step forward, each decision made in favor of your well-being, and each day you choose your happiness over your history is a testament to your strength. Document these achievements, look back on them, and let them serve as reminders of your capability and courage.

It's also beneficial to **connect with others who share similar experiences**. Engaging with fellow survivors can validate your feelings and help you see that survival is not just possible but is a reality you're living. These connections can foster a sense of community and collective resilience, reinforcing the idea that you're not alone in your journey.

To find the strength for this, you need to **embrace empowerment**. Empowerment comes from making choices that align with your best interests, asserting your needs, and setting boundaries that protect your mental and emotional health. It's about taking control of your narrative and owning every part of your story—both the struggles and the triumphs. Embracing empowerment means standing in your truth, knowing that you have the power to define who you are and how you live your life, unchained from the shadows of the past. This empowerment is the cornerstone of crafting and owning your survival story—a narrative that honors your journey and resilience.

Creating Your Survivor Narrative

One effective method to create and solidify your survivor narrative is through writing exercises. Start by **writing a letter to your past self** during a particularly challenging time. Offer the compassion, encouragement, and advice you wish you had received then. This can help you see how far you've come and affirm that the challenges you faced have contributed to your strength and wisdom.

Visualization techniques also play a crucial role in embracing empowerment. Spend a few minutes each day closing your eyes and imagining your life as you wish it to be. Visualize yourself achieving your goals, feeling happy, safe, and fulfilled. See yourself as the protagonist of your story who overcomes adversity. This practice boosts your mood and strengthens your belief in your ability to create the life you envision.

Additionally, **creating a vision board** can help manifest your survivor narrative into something tangible. Use images, quotes, and symbols that represent your goals, dreams, and the identity you are building. Placing this board somewhere you can see it daily serves as a constant reminder of your path and the future you are actively constructing.

Crafting your survival story isn't just about acknowledging the past—it's also about writing the next chapters of your life with intention and courage. Each word you write and each image you visualize adds depth to your story, transforming it from a tale of survival to one of thriving.

Embrace this process as a powerful declaration of your autonomy and strength. This is your story, your life, and every step you take is a testament to your resilience and your power to shape your destiny.

SETTING BOUNDARIES: THE ULTIMATE ACT OF SELF-RESPECT

Setting boundaries is an essential act of self-care and respect. It's about clearly defining what is acceptable and what isn't in your relationships and your life. By establishing boundaries, you honor your own needs and feelings, asserting your right to emotional and psychological well-being. This process involves taking stock of past interactions and identifying areas where your limits were not respected or where you felt compromised.

To begin, reflect on the areas of your life where you feel drained or uncomfortable—these sensations often indicate where boundaries are needed. For instance, if you find yourself overwhelmed by social obligations, setting limits on your social engagements can help preserve your energy. If you feel undervalued at work, it might be necessary to assert your need for proper recognition or to define the scope of your professional responsibilities more clearly.

Also, consider your emotional boundaries. Pay attention to situations where you feel pressured to share more than you're comfortable with or engage in emotional labor that leaves you depleted. Recognizing these patterns is the first step toward changing them.

Once you identify where boundaries are needed, the next challenge is to uphold them, which is crucial for your recovery and ongoing mental health. This might include saying no to additional responsibilities that conflict with your recovery goals or choosing not to engage with individuals who consistently disregard your feelings and needs.

Communicating Boundaries

How exactly do you communicate those boundaries? It's one thing to identify where they need to be set but articulating them to others is a whole different challenge—one that's crucial for your well-being. Effective communication of your boundaries is key to ensuring they are respected and maintained.

Start by being clear and direct. When you express your boundaries, use "I" statements to make it personal and less accusative. For example, say, "I feel overwhelmed when we discuss this topic, so I need to avoid it for now," instead of "You overwhelm me when you talk about this." This approach makes your message about your needs and feelings rather than the behavior of the other person.

Be assertive but calm. Assertiveness is about respecting yourself and others; it's not about being aggressive. You're simply stating your needs respectfully and standing firm on them. Practice what you want to say beforehand if it helps you feel more confident. Remember, setting boundaries isn't a negotiation; it's a declaration of your needs.

Timing is also essential. Choose a moment to discuss your boundaries when you're not already emotionally charged from a recent conflict. A calm, neutral time allows both parties to be more receptive and less defensive.

Explain why the boundary is important to you. This can help the other person understand your perspective and the significance of respecting your boundary. For instance, "I need to have some quiet time in the evenings because it helps me unwind from my day. I would appreciate it if we could keep social calls to earlier in the afternoon."

After you've communicated your boundaries, it's crucial to maintain them. Consistency is key. If you give mixed signals by not adhering to your own boundaries, it might confuse others and lead them to test or disregard your limits. So, you need to ensure you honor your own boundaries as diligently as you expect others to. Maintaining your boundaries teaches others how to treat you and reinforces your own sense of self-worth and respect. It's a fundamental part of building a healthy, balanced life where your needs are met, and your relationships are fulfilling. Finally, remember that it's also your responsibility to respect the boundaries of others. This reciprocal understanding can foster mutual respect and improve your relationships.

REDISCOVERING JOY AND PASSION: CULTIVATING PERSONAL INTERESTS

We've touched before on how reconnecting to personal interests can ignite the spark of recovery and self-discovery. Engaging in activities that bring you joy is not just a pastime —it's a profound act of healing. Each moment spent in personal enjoyment is a step away from the shadows of abuse and a step toward reclaiming your life. Viewing your personal joy and fulfillment as acts of resistance against the abuse endured can transform everyday activities into powerful statements of self-affirmation.

When you participate in activities you love, whether they're artistic, physical, intellectual, or simply leisurely, you send a message to yourself and the world: I am here, I am whole, and I am more than my past experiences. These interests anchor you in the present and allow you to experience moments of pure being, unattached to any external validation or influence.

Moreover, these interests often reconnect you to a community with similar passions. This can be incredibly uplifting and can further help dilute the lingering effects of isolation that often accompany abusive relationships. Being part of a community provides a sense of belonging and support, reinforcing that you are not alone in your journey.

Personal interests also foster a sense of competence and growth. Learning a new skill or deepening your understanding of a beloved hobby can boost your confidence and help rebuild the self-esteem that was eroded by abuse. Each new achievement, no matter how small, is a building block in the new foundation of your self-worth.

Reconnecting With Old Interests

Revisiting previous hobbies and interests that were set aside can be like reconnecting with old friends; it's comforting, familiar, and often incredibly healing. These activities, whether they were creative endeavors, athletic pursuits, or intellectual projects, once brought joy and a sense of fulfillment to your life. By revisiting them, you not only reignite those feelings but also reclaim a part of yourself that may have been lost in the chaos of abusive dynamics.

Start by **making a list** of the things you used to love doing before your experiences led you to push them aside. Did you enjoy painting or drawing? Perhaps you found solace in playing a musical instrument, writing poetry, or hiking through nature. Maybe it was a weekly cooking class, a book club, or gardening. Whatever those activities were, write them down.

Then, **take small, manageable steps** to reintegrate these activities into your life. If you used to love to paint, start with a simple, no-pressure project. If you were a runner, begin with short, leisurely walks and gradually reintroduce yourself to running. The key here is to proceed without pressure or expectations. Allow yourself to enjoy the process, even if it feels a bit rusty at first. The goal is to find joy and a sense of normalcy in these activities again.

As you engage with these old hobbies, pay attention to how you feel. It's normal to experience a mix of emotions, from nostalgia to relief or even sadness for the time lost. These feelings are all valid and part of the healing journey. Embracing them without judgment can lead to profound personal insights and growth.

Exploring New Passions

Once you've reestablished a connection with your former interests, you'll likely find your confidence and curiosity growing. This renewed sense of self can be a powerful catalyst for exploring new avenues of joy and passion. Embracing new activities can open doors to worlds you might never have considered before, enriching your life with fresh experiences and perspectives.

Now is the perfect time to stretch your boundaries and try something completely different. Whether it's a sport, an artistic endeavor, or a new hobby like pottery or photography, each new activity provides a unique opportunity to discover facets of yourself that are yet unexplored. Engaging in these new passions allows you to redefine your life on your own terms, giving you a sense of control and accomplishment.

As you continue on this path of rediscovery and healing, remember that this journey involves a variety of strategies beyond just exploring new interests. In the next chapter, we will learn about other essential tools and techniques that support healing. Together, these strategies form a comprehensive approach to healing, empowering you to move forward with resilience, fulfillment, and autonomy.

4

TOOLS AND TECHNIQUES FOR HEALING

> *"You can't hate yourself into change. Love yourself into greatness."*
>
> — *EMMA LOVEWELL*

One evening, after a particularly grueling day, I found myself with a journal in my lap and a pen in my hand. The emotions I'd been bottling up needed an outlet, and words began to flow as freely as the tears down my cheeks. I wrote so much that my hand ached, but with each page, I felt a weight lifting. By the time I set the pen down, the emotional release was palpable—I was exhausted yet inexplicably lighter. It was a simple practice, journaling, yet its impact was profound, teaching me the power of expressing the unspoken.

In this chapter, we're going to explore various healing practices that might seem simple at first glance but are incredibly potent in the healing process. These tools—some of which we have touched on—can be gateways to deeper self-understanding and recovery.

Each one of them offers unique benefits and can be tailored to fit where you are in your healing journey. Perhaps you'll find solace in the quiet reflection of journaling or the structured support of therapy. Maybe the collective strength found in support groups will resonate with you or the grounding presence mindfulness brings to your daily life.

As we explore these practices, I encourage you to consider which ones feel right for you at this moment. Which are you ready to try? Which might you save for another time? Remember, this journey is uniquely yours, and choosing the tools that best suit your path is a crucial step toward healing and rediscovery.

THE POWER OF MINDFULNESS: STAYING GROUNDED IN THE PRESENT

When I first encountered the concept of mindfulness, I was skeptical. How could simply "being in the moment'" mend the deep-seated scars left by years of emotional turbulence? Yet, as I began to weave mindfulness practices into my daily routine, I noticed a profound shift. The anxious thoughts and the shadows of past traumas started losing their grip on me, moment by moment.

Mindfulness is essentially about presence. It's the practice of anchoring yourself in the present moment, recognizing and accepting your feelings, thoughts, and bodily sensations without judgment. For those of us recovering from narcissistic abuse, this practice can be particularly life-changing. It helps shift our focus from painful memories and worries about the future to what is happening right now. This shift doesn't erase the pain but can lessen its intensity, making it more manageable.

Integrating mindfulness into your daily routine can significantly enhance your emotional stability and peace. It can be as simple as starting your day with a five-minute breathing exercise, where you focus solely on the rhythm of your breath—inhaling peace and exhaling tension. It could also involve a practice known as "mindful walking," where you consciously note each step, the feel of the ground under your feet, the sounds around you, and the air on your skin during the walk.

For survivors of abuse, specific mindfulness exercises can be especially beneficial. One such exercise is the **body scan** (Gibson, 2019). This involves lying down in a quiet space and slowly bringing your attention to different parts of your body. As you focus on each area, notice any sensations, pain, or discomfort without trying to change these feelings. This practice can help reconnect you with your body, which is often neglected or dissociated from, during times of psychological stress.

Another helpful practice is **mindful listening** (Gibson, 2019). This can be done by listening to a piece of music or the sounds of nature, focusing entirely on the different sounds and the emotions they evoke. This exercise helps draw your attention away from distressing thoughts and toward a calming, focusing activity.

Remember, the key to mindfulness is regular practice. It's not about perfection or achieving a state of constant calm, but about increasing your awareness and presence gradually over time. Each moment of mindfulness is a step toward reclaiming your mental space from the intrusive thoughts planted by past abuse. It's about giving yourself permission to pause, to breathe, and to be present in each moment, affirming that you are here, you are alive, and you are whole.

JOURNALING FOR EMOTIONAL RELEASE: WRITING AS A FORM OF THERAPY

Remember when I mentioned my intense journaling experience? That wasn't just a one-off event; it became a vital part of my healing journey. Journaling can be a form of therapy, providing a safe space to express emotions, unpack thoughts, and document the healing process.

The act of putting pen to paper allows you to articulate feelings that might be too complex or painful to speak out loud. It can be a profound tool for emotional processing and release. Each entry helps to declutter your mind, transferring the turmoil inside onto a neutral, external space where it can be examined with less bias. This process can illuminate patterns and triggers, offering insights that might be missed in the swirl of daily thoughts.

Using journaling to track both your progress and setbacks can be incredibly rewarding. Over time, flipping through past pages can reveal just how far you've come, which is incredibly encouraging on days when it feels like you're stuck. It shows that healing isn't linear, but a path marked by peaks and valleys, each significant in its own right.

To help navigate your feelings and thoughts, here are some targeted journal prompts:

- What feelings am I holding onto today that I need to let go of?
- Write a letter to my past self at a critical moment of abuse, offering the support and wisdom I needed then.
- List five qualities I've rediscovered in myself since beginning my recovery journey.
- Describe a recent situation where I recognized and avoided a potential trigger.
- What does forgiveness mean to me in the context of my recovery, and how can I work toward it at my own pace?

Creating a journaling practice that feels safe and private is crucial. Choose a journal that resonates with you, one that you're drawn to physically—this can be a bound book, a digital document, or even a series of voice recordings. Keep it in a place where you feel it's secure, whether that's locked away or hidden in a special spot only you know about.

When you journal, allow yourself to write freely. Don't worry about grammar or style. The important thing is honesty and emotional truth. By honesty, I mean being factual and straightforward about the events or situations in your life. Emotional truth, on the other hand, involves expressing how these events make you feel—allowing yourself to explore and articulate your true emotional responses without judgment or censorship. This means you aim to be clear and truthful about what's happening while also diving deep into your personal emotional experience of those events. If privacy concerns you, consider developing a code or shorthand only you understand or use digital tools that offer encryption.

Remember, this journal is for you and you alone. It's a place to be unapologetically honest, question, cry, rage, and ultimately, heal. Each word you write down is a step toward understanding yourself better and rebuilding the life you envision.

CREATIVE EXPRESSION: HEALING THROUGH ART, MUSIC, AND DANCE

Creative expression has been an incredible part of my healing journey, and it's something I've come to cherish. The beauty of using art, music, and dance in recovery is that you don't need to be an artist, a musician, or a dancer to benefit from these activities. It's not about creating a masterpiece but rather about letting your emotions flow through a different medium, giving voice to feelings that words sometimes can't capture.

Art, in its many forms, offers a unique therapeutic advantage (Shukla et al., 2022). It allows you to externalize what's internal, making abstract emotions tangible. When you paint, sketch, or mold clay, you're essentially processing emotions through your hands. Each color or line can represent a different aspect of your experience, helping you to visualize and confront these in a safe, controlled environment.

Similarly, music can be a powerful healer. Whether you're playing an instrument, singing, or simply listening, music has the ability to bypass the rational brain and reach straight into the emotional core. Certain songs or rhythms can resonate with our feelings, helping to release pent-up emotions or offering solace through lyrics that feel as though they were written just for us.

Dance, too, is a profound form of expression. It combines physical activity with emotional expression, making it a dual force against stress and anxiety. Moving your body to music can be liberating, helping to shake off the weight of your worries and restore a sense of freedom and lightness.

If you're new to creative expression, the key is to explore different mediums to find what resonates with you. You might start with something simple, like doodling or coloring in an adult coloring book. These activities don't require any artistic skills but can still provide a therapeutic outlet. Or perhaps you might create a playlist of music that speaks to your journey, listening to it when you feel the need to connect with your emotions.

Another accessible entry point could be attending a dance class or even just allowing yourself to move freely to music at home. There is no shortage of free dance tutorial videos online if carving out time or financial resources don't allow for attending a class in person. Notice how different types of music influence your mood and movement. The idea is to let go of any judgment and allow yourself to be in the moment, experiencing the healing benefits of pure expression.

The goal of using creative expression for healing isn't to produce something worthy of exhibition or performance; it's about the process itself. It's about making space for your emotions, playing with them, and letting them out in a way that can be both healing and incredibly personal. So, give yourself permission to explore and express yourself creatively; you might be surprised by what you discover about yourself.

BUILDING A SELF-CARE ROUTINE: PRIORITIZING YOUR WELL-BEING

Self-care is often pictured as spa days or indulgent treats, but it's so much more—it's any activity that nurtures your well-being. For those of us healing from trauma, self-care becomes a vital foundation, helping to sustain our mental health over the long haul.

Consistency in self-care is key. It's not just about doing something nice for yourself occasionally; it's about making regular practices that support your health and happiness. This consistency helps create a buffer against the daily stresses and the emotional upheavals that come with recovery from abuse.

Developing a personal self-care plan involves looking at your needs across three broad areas: physical, emotional, and spiritual. Physically, it might mean setting regular sleep patterns, engaging in physical activity, or managing your diet in ways that energize rather than drain you. Emotionally, it could involve practices like journaling, therapy sessions, or creative activities that allow you to express and process your feelings. Spiritually, you might find strength in meditation, spending time in nature, or exploring your personal beliefs and values.

An often-overlooked aspect of self-care is setting boundaries. Learning to say no is a profound form of self-care. It's about respecting your limits and not allowing yourself to be overwhelmed or taken advantage of. It's crucial to recognize that you have the right to protect your energy and peace. Setting boundaries might mean declining invitations that don't feel right, stepping back from relationships that drain you, or simply giving yourself permission to rest without feeling guilty.

Here are a few steps to start building your self-care routine:

- Identify what drains you and what replenishes you. Make a list of all the activities and people in your life that contribute to your stress and those that help you feel recharged.
- Set clear boundaries. Based on your list, begin to establish boundaries that help protect your energy. Communicate these boundaries clearly and respectfully to those around you.
- Schedule regular self-care time. Whether it's a daily 10-minute meditation or a weekly art class, make self-care a non-negotiable part of your schedule.

Begin incorporating those steps into your routine slowly and adjust as you learn what works best for you. Some days will be harder than others, and that's okay. Self-care is not about perfection; it's about making a consistent effort to take care of your well-being.

THE ROLE OF THERAPY: SEEKING PROFESSIONAL GUIDANCE

When I first considered therapy, I carried a heavy load of stigma about seeking mental health support. There was a part of me that felt like asking for help meant admitting a kind of defeat. But as I navigated the aftermath of the toxicity of a narcissistic partner, I realized that reaching out wasn't a sign of weakness; it was a step toward reclaiming my strength.

There are various types of therapy and counseling available that can be incredibly beneficial for survivors of narcissistic abuse. **Cognitive behavioral therapy (CBT)** is particularly effective, as it helps identify and change the negative thought patterns that can be remnants of abusive relationships. Trauma-focused therapy, such as **Eye movement desensitization and reprocessing (EMDR)**, can also be profoundly healing, helping to process and integrate traumatic memories safely (Laderer, 2023).

Building a trusting relationship with a therapist is crucial for effective healing. It's important to feel understood and safe. When searching for a therapist, look for someone who specializes in narcissistic abuse or has experience with trauma. In your initial sessions, observe how you feel: Are you being heard? Do you feel respected and validated? Trust your instincts; the right therapist should make you feel supported and empowered.

I encourage anyone hesitant about seeking therapy to keep an open mind. The stigma surrounding mental health is slowly being dismantled, and there is immense strength in allowing yourself to receive help. Therapy can provide you with tools and insights that are hard to access on your own.

Additionally, therapy doesn't have to be the only method in your healing journey. It can be combined with other practices like the mindfulness and journaling we discussed, creating a holistic recovery process. For instance, you might find that mindfulness helps manage anxiety between sessions, while journaling can be a way to continue exploring your emotions on your own time.

In my experience, blending therapy with other healing modalities helped create a balanced and personalized recovery strategy. It allowed me not only to heal from my past but also to build a new future with greater resilience and understanding. The journey isn't always easy, but the right support can lead to transformative growth and a deeper sense of peace.

SUPPORT GROUPS: FINDING STRENGTH IN SHARED STORIES

Participating in support groups where members share similar experiences provides immense emotional and psychological benefits. In these groups, every story shared is a reminder that you are not alone in your struggles. Hearing others articulate their feelings and experiences can validate your own, often giving you words for emotions you couldn't quite describe yourself. This validation is crucial—it's a powerful antidote to the isolation that often comes with surviving narcissistic abuse. Being part of a community that understands what you've been through fosters a sense of belonging and acceptance that can be hard to find elsewhere.

The support group acts as a sanctuary where emotions and thoughts can be expressed freely and without judgment. This safe space is essential for healing and growth. In my experience, the acts of sharing and listening are therapeutic. It's comforting to speak with others who understand what you're going through without needing to explain or justify your feelings.

Finding a supportive and safe group, whether online or in person, requires some consideration. Start by defining what you need most from a group. Are you looking for empathy, shared experiences, coping strategies, or all of the above? Once you know what you need, search for groups that focus on these areas. Many organizations offer directories of support groups by topic or demographic.

For example, the Anxiety and Depression Association of America provides a list of groups for those dealing with mood disorders, while local community centers often host groups for new parents or recovering addicts. Online forums and social media platforms can also be good starting points, with sites like Reddit and Facebook offering a variety of special-interest groups where you can find others dealing with similar issues. Remember to attend a few meetings before deciding if a group suits you, as each group's dynamics are unique.

It's important to maintain personal boundaries in these settings. While it's beneficial to share and connect, remember to share only what you feel comfortable with. It's okay to be a listener until you feel ready to open up. Setting these boundaries can protect your emotional well-being and make your experience in a support group more positive.

AFFIRMATIONS FOR SELF-WORTH: DAILY MANTRAS FOR EMPOWERMENT

Affirmations can be amazing tools in reshaping thought patterns and self-beliefs, particularly for those healing from emotional abuse. These powerful statements are designed to foster a positive mindset and reinforce the inherent worth that everyone possesses, regardless of their past experiences.

Crafting personal affirmations involves reflecting on your specific needs and the aspects of self-worth you wish to strengthen. To create affirmations that resonate with your personal journey, start by identifying negative beliefs or frequent criticisms that you've internalized over time. Turn each negative thought into a positive statement that reflects the truth about your value and capabilities. For example, if you often think, "I am not good enough," transform that into, "I am worthy just as I am."

Here are some steps to help you craft impactful affirmations:

- **Be positive:** Frame your affirmations in a positive tone, focusing on what you want to feel, not what you want to avoid.
- **Keep it in the present tense:** Even if you don't fully believe the statement yet, affirming it as if it's already true helps you start to accept it as reality.
- **Make it specific:** General affirmations are less effective. Tailor your statements to address your specific desires and needs.

- **Use your own voice:** The affirmation should sound like you. If it's too formal or just doesn't feel like something you would say, it's less likely to impact your thoughts.

To incorporate affirmations into your daily routine, consider setting aside a few moments each morning to repeat them aloud. You might also write them on sticky notes and place them where you'll see them throughout the day, such as on your bathroom mirror or the dashboard of your car. Some find it helpful to create a daily reminder on their phone to pause and mentally recite their affirmations. This was particularly helpful for me, as sometimes my workday would simply get away from me. A mid-morning and mid-afternoon reset were welcomed and often changed my mood and productivity.

Recognizing the impact of these affirmations on your self-esteem and outlook can be uplifting. Over time, you may notice a shift in how you respond to challenges and negative thoughts. Instead of being overwhelmed by doubt, you might find yourself empowered by a new, positive narrative about your capabilities and worth.

For those who are looking for some examples of effective affirmations, the final chapter of this book provides a selection that can be adapted to various needs and stages of recovery. Sometimes a ready-made list helps someone at the beginner level to bypass the stumbling block of crafting their own. This helps with eliminating procrastination and allows you to jump right in.

Moving forward, the next chapter will explore nurturing resilience and inner strength. We will learn about embracing vulnerability, overcoming fear, and trusting in ourselves—a vital continuation of the journey you are on. Each step forward with affirmations paves the way for deeper work on building the robust and resilient self that can thrive despite past adversities.

PAY IT FORWARD BY SHARING YOUR THOUGHTS

Dear Readers,

Your perspective on this book is invaluable in helping other women understand it's impact. Whether you are finding solace in the advice, discovering useful strategies, or simply resonating with the experiences shared, your feedback can be a guiding light for another woman going through a similar situation.

How to Pay it Forward:

1. Scan the below QR code to access the review form.
2. Share your honest thoughts on the book – what you liked, what resonated with you, and any advice you found particularly helpful.
3. Rate the book based on your overall experience.

By collecting your reviews, I aim to create a community of support for those navigating the aftermath of high-conflict divorces. Thank you for taking the time to share your thoughts and contribute to our community. Your review can make a real difference!

Warm regards,

Daphne Rice

5

NURTURING RESILIENCE AND INNER STRENGTH

"If we all did the things we are capable of doing, we would literally astound ourselves."

— *THOMAS EDISON*

Trusting myself again was perhaps one of the most challenging hurdles I faced on my journey to recovery. After years of living in a reality distorted by gaslighting, I found my inner voice had been drowned out by the overwhelming din of doubt and manipulation. It was as if I had to learn anew what it meant to listen to my own instincts, to trust my own feelings and perceptions.

Rebuilding that trust didn't happen overnight. It was a process fraught with moments of self-doubt and self-recrimination. Yes, I made mistakes—as everyone does—but I learned that acknowledging those mistakes didn't mean I had to shoulder all the blame for everything that went wrong. It meant learning from them, allowing them to teach me, and most importantly, it meant learning to distinguish between genuine missteps and the false narratives that had been imposed upon me.

This chapter is about nurturing resilience and inner strength, about embracing the vulnerability that comes with examining and overcoming our fears. It's about how to start trusting ourselves deeply, even when our past experiences have conditioned us to do otherwise.

Cultivating resilience is about more than just bouncing back; it's about growing through our challenges, about turning adversity into a catalyst for growth. It involves opening ourselves up to our vulnerabilities, acknowledging them, and using them as a foundation to build a stronger, more assured self.

As we explore these themes, I invite you to join me in peeling back the layers of fear and self-doubt to reveal the core of who you are. It's there—in the quiet assurance of your own worth—that you'll find the strength to trust yourself again, stand firm in your beliefs and convictions, and move forward with confidence. Let's take this path together, learning how to harness our inner strengths to forge a resilient, empowered future.

CULTIVATING RESILIENCE

Cultivating resilience is a crucial aspect of our human experience. It's about developing the mental and emotional toughness to face and overcome adversities, which in turn fortifies us for future challenges. However, it's vital to clarify that while resilience involves facing hardships, it doesn't mean romanticizing suffering. We all have our limits, and recognizing these is as important as pushing beyond them.

To build resilience, we must first acknowledge and accept the adversities we face. This doesn't mean we should seek out hardship or tolerate unacceptable situations, but rather learn from the challenges that life inevitably throws our way. Each difficulty we overcome teaches us something new about our strengths and capabilities, deepening our understanding of ourselves and enhancing our ability to handle stress.

Strategies to maintain resilience involve:

- **Self-awareness:** Recognize your emotional responses to stress and understand the sources of these emotions. Self-awareness is the first step toward managing your reactions effectively.
- **Healthy relationships:** Cultivate a supportive network. Having people who provide encouragement and perspective can be a tremendous source of strength in tough times.
- **Acceptance:** Sometimes, part of resilience is acknowledging that some situations cannot be changed and learning to live with that reality. Acceptance can help you focus your energy on things that you can influence.
- **Self-care:** Regularly engage in activities that replenish your energy and decrease stress. This can include physical activities, hobbies, or relaxation techniques.
- **Goal-setting:** Establishing realistic, attainable goals

provides a sense of purpose and a direction that can guide you through adversity.

- **Optimism:** Maintaining a hopeful outlook is a key part of resilience. This doesn't mean ignoring the less pleasant aspects of life but rather focusing on the positives and working with a belief that things can improve (Hurley, 2024).

It's also important to know when to seek help. Resilience doesn't mean going it alone; reaching out for support when it's needed can be a powerful step toward recovery.

In embracing these strategies, we fortify ourselves not just to bounce back but to bounce forward. We learn that our experiences, even the painful ones, contribute to our growth and make us more robust. Let's carry these lessons forward, allowing them to shape a resilient mindset that empowers us to face future challenges with confidence.

THE STRENGTH OF VULNERABILITY: EMBRACING YOUR EMOTIONAL DEPTH

Challenging the notion that vulnerability is a weakness has been a profound part of my healing journey. For a long time, vulnerability felt like a dangerous territory, a place where you could be hurt, manipulated, or worse. However, I've come to understand that embracing vulnerability is not about exposing yourself to harm; it's about acknowledging your emotions and allowing yourself to truly connect with others.

Embracing vulnerability allows us to express our genuine selves. It's about letting down those walls we've built to protect ourselves and instead opening up to the possibility of deeper, more meaningful relationships. When we share our true feelings, thoughts, and fears, we make it possible for others to see us as we really are. This authenticity invites a kind of intimacy that superficial interactions simply cannot achieve.

Moreover, being open about our struggles and weaknesses can significantly accelerate our healing process. It creates space for emotional release and helps us process our experiences more thoroughly. By acknowledging and expressing our vulnerabilities, we can work through our emotions rather than bottling them up where they can fester and lead to greater distress.

However, embracing vulnerability doesn't mean we should leave ourselves unprotected. It's crucial to balance openness with measures that ensure our emotional safety. This means being selective about whom we choose to open up to, ensuring they are trustworthy and supportive. It also involves setting clear boundaries about what we are and are not willing to share and stepping back if we feel overwhelmed or unsafe.

OVERCOMING FEAR OF THE FUTURE:
STRATEGIES FOR HOPE AND OPTIMISM

So far, we've explored a variety of strategies, tools, and techniques for healing alongside the critical roles of resilience and vulnerability. As we continue our journey, it's essential to address one of the more common obstacles many of us face after enduring past trauma: the fear of the future. This fear can manifest as a looming shadow, casting doubt on our hopes and plans, often holding us back from fully embracing the life we deserve.

Identifying your specific fears about the future is the first step toward overcoming them. These fears might include worries about repeating past mistakes, concerns about financial stability, or anxiety over future relationships. Understanding where these fears originate—be it past disappointments, trauma, or external influences—can illuminate why we feel the way we do and how we can start to address these fears constructively.

To overcome these fears, here are some strategies that have been instrumental in my journey:

- **Acknowledge and accept your fears:** Recognition is the first step toward change. By acknowledging your fears, you give yourself the power to tackle them head-on. I remember the evening I sat down, journal in hand, and wrote out all the fears that had been clouding my mind. It was an emotional process but seeing them on paper somehow made them less intimidating.
- **Break fears down into manageable parts:** Large, undefined fears are more challenging to confront. Break them down into smaller, specific concerns that you can address one at a time. For instance, rather than overwhelming myself with the fear of failing in my career post-divorce, I started by setting small, achievable goals each week to rebuild my professional confidence.
- **Use positive visualization:** Imagine the best possible outcomes instead of the worst. Visualization can help

reframe your mindset to expect success rather than anticipate failure. Each morning, I would spend a few minutes visualizing a day where I felt accomplished and acknowledged, which slowly began to shift my expectations from dread to optimism.

- **Develop a plan:** Sometimes, our fears about the future are rooted in feeling unprepared. Developing a clear plan for your goals can provide a road map and reduce anxiety about the unknown. I outlined steps to enhance my skills and network, which provided a clear path forward and significantly lessened my anxiety about professional stability.

Remember, the future holds as much promise as uncertainty. By applying the healing techniques we've learned, like mindfulness and journaling, and by continuing to embrace our vulnerability and resilience, we can approach the future not as a threat but as a canvas of possibilities waiting to be painted with our renewed hopes and dreams.

Through these strategies, I managed to quell the immediate fears that once seemed insurmountable and built a foundation of resilience that prepared me for future challenges. This journey of overcoming fear is continuous, and with each step, I gather more strength and assurance, ready to face whatever comes next with a renewed spirit and optimistic outlook.

TRUSTING YOURSELF AGAIN: THE FOUNDATION OF INNER STRENGTH

Finally, all the strategies we've absorbed culminate in one of the most vital steps of our journey: learning to trust ourselves again. This step isn't just about recovery; it's about laying the groundwork for a future where we stand strong and secure in our decisions and judgments.

Remember at the beginning of this chapter when I mentioned that rebuilding my trust was a difficult process? I had to study a lot about the actual condition of narcissism, read past messages, journaling, and notes, and ask friends to help develop the most realistic version of the truth. That was when I started to believe that while, yes, I made my mistakes, I wasn't to blame for the most part. I am someone who readily blames myself for other people's mistakes. I think, *Well, it is my fault I let this happen in the first place*, but this is just unfair.

This self-blame is a common trap for many survivors, ingrained from cycles of manipulation where the abuser often shifts the blame, making us feel responsible for the chaos and hurt in the relationship.

Self-trust is the cornerstone of confidence in our decision-making and personal judgment. After the distortions and manipulations of narcissistic abuse, regaining this trust means reconnecting with and relying on our own intuition. It's about believing in our ability to make sound decisions and respecting our own boundaries without second-guessing ourselves.

As I worked through this process, piecing together my own narrative from the distorted one I had been given, I realized the power of owning my story. This wasn't just about dissecting the past; it was about laying a new foundation for the future—a future where I trust my judgments and feel secure in my choices. Reestablishing this trust in myself has been liberating, allowing me to move forward with clarity and resilience.

Here's how we can start rebuilding this crucial trust:

- **Validate your emotions:** Recognize and honor your feelings. This acknowledgment is a fundamental step toward respecting your inner voice.
- **Reflect on your resilience:** Think back to moments when you successfully navigated challenges. Reminding yourself of these instances can reinforce your confidence in your ability to trust your own decisions.
- **Define your limits:** Establishing clear limits is essential after experiencing manipulation. It involves determining what you are and aren't comfortable with in various aspects of your life. Start to live by these rules as a fundamental exercise in trusting and respecting your own needs and boundaries.
- **Forgive yourself:** Learning to forgive yourself for past mistakes is part of this process. Acknowledge that everyone makes mistakes and use them as learning opportunities rather than reasons for self-criticism. This approach not only helps in setting realistic boundaries but also in building self-

compassion and trust in your decision-making capabilities.

- **Gradually reduce external dependencies:** While feedback from trusted friends or therapists can be helpful, aim to gradually rely more on your own judgment. This shift reinforces internal trust over external validation.

By focusing on these steps, we begin rebuilding the trust in ourselves that was eroded by past abuse. This renewed self-trust forms a robust foundation for our futures, empowering us to flourish independently, excel in our roles as single mothers, and relish solitude if that's our choice. It emboldens us to make decisions that resonate with our true selves without fear or doubt shadowing our paths.

In the forthcoming chapter, we will learn how we can harness this reclaimed trust to transform our lives fundamentally. We'll look at practical ways to apply our inner confidence and self-reliance to face challenges head-on, pursue goals with conviction, and create a life that's not just about enduring but about thriving in every sense. This exploration will equip us with strategies to enhance our resilience, celebrate our independence, and ensure that we lead lives marked by joy and fulfillment wholly on our own terms.

6

BUILDING A NEW LIFE

> *"The difference between try and triumph is a little 'umph'."*

— MARVIN PHILLIPS— MARVIN PHILLIPS

When I first faced the prospect of caring for my children alone, my heart was a mix of fear and uncertainty. Nights stretched long with worries about how I could possibly provide the warmth and security of a two-parent household by myself. Would I be enough for them? Could I create a nurturing environment where they could thrive?

Yet, as the days turned into weeks and months, I found a reservoir of strength I didn't know I possessed. It was through the quiet moments of solitude, once the children were in bed and the house was silent, that I started to embrace my new reality. Solitude became my sanctuary for reflection and growth. It was in these quiet hours that I discovered the resilience to sustain my family and the creativity to enrich our lives.

I learned to turn our home into a safe haven, a place where laughter filled the rooms and where each challenge we faced became a stepping-stone to something greater. We explored new traditions and built our unique routines, and I watched my children adapt and flourish, their resilience matching my own.

Through this journey, I realized that my initial fears, while valid, were not insurmountable. They transformed into a deep-seated determination to maintain and enhance our lives. Our home—once a symbol of what I feared I couldn't provide—became the very place where we all thrived.

Sharing this story isn't just about recounting my struggles and victories; it's about offering hope and reassurance. If you're standing where I once was, know that you, too, have the strength to build a nurturing, thriving environment for your family. Embrace the solitude that comes with solo parenting; let it teach you, strengthen you, and lead you to discover the boundless love and resilience that lies within.

SOLO PARENTING: THRIVING AS A SINGLE MOTHER

Remember in Chapter 1 when we discussed how narcissistic abuse can shake our confidence as mothers? We discussed the critical need to protect our children and foster an open communication atmosphere to rebuild our confidence in motherhood. We emphasized the importance of teaching our kids about emotional intelligence and creating a supportive,

BUILDING A NEW LIFE | 101

nurturing home for their emotional and psychological growth. These elements are the bedrock of rebuilding and thriving as a solo parent.

Thriving as a single mother doesn't come with a manual. It's a journey—one that requires patience, resilience, and a whole lot of love. From the early days of solo parenting, establishing a routine has been a lifeline for us. It provides a sense of security and predictability, which is especially comforting to children who have experienced the instability of a tumultuous relationship. Whether it's the bedtime stories that whisk us away to magical lands or our Wednesday pizza nights—these rituals anchor us. They give my children consistency in a world that has often felt inconsistent. And isn't that what we all crave? A bit of predictability amidst the chaos?

Self-Care for Single Parents

Amid these routines, it's crucial for us, as solo parents, to remember the vital role of self-care. It's easy to get caught up in the daily hustle of parenting, work, and household duties. However, taking time for ourselves isn't a luxury—it's essential. Self-care is the fuel that keeps our engines running smoothly, preventing burnout and ensuring we can be the best we can be for our children.

Think of self-care as an investment in your family's well-being as well as your own. It can be as simple as taking fifteen minutes to sip your morning coffee in silence, a quick midday walk, or an occasional night out with friends. These moments of pause are not just breaks from routine but are vital in maintaining our mental and emotional health.

Incorporating these practices helps us manage stress and preserve our energy. It reinforces our emotional resilience, enabling us to handle the challenges of solo parenting with greater ease and grace. When we care for ourselves, we model healthy habits for our children, too—they learn the importance of self-respect and personal well-being through our actions.

In the next chapter, we will explore in greater depth the role of physical health, nutrition, and stress management techniques. These elements are integral to sustaining our overall health and enhancing our ability to thrive as solo parents.

Building a Support Network

Building or strengthening a support network is essential, especially for us solo parents. Remember, being a solo parent doesn't mean we have to go it alone. When I finalized my divorce, one of the thoughts that often circled my mind was how I could cultivate a circle of support that wasn't just about logistical help but also provided genuine emotional backing. It hit me that while I was parenting solo, I certainly didn't need to be completely "solo" in navigating life.

Creating a strong network started with me reaching out, which felt daunting at first, especially being accustomed to managing everything on my own. But I took small steps, connecting with other parents at school events, chatting with neighbors, and reconnecting with old friends. These connections became my lifeline—people who could share the load of a ride to school, join us for a combined family dinner, or just lend an ear when the days felt overwhelmingly long.

I also found comfort and camaraderie with support groups. Meeting others in similar situations, both in person and online, became a cornerstone of my new life. We shared stories, exchanged advice, and supported each other through ups and downs. It was relieving to find a community where I felt understood, a place where our shared experiences brought us together, making the journey of solo parenting less lonely.

Volunteering at my children's school and local community events further broadened my social circle. It was a step into the community that also paved the way for my children and me to make new friends and build supportive relationships. These experiences not only enriched our lives but also showed us the strength of community bonds.

Considering new relationships was another significant step. Embracing the idea of new partnerships was a testament to my healing, and truthfully did not happen for years. It wasn't about rushing into something new but about being open to the possibility of adding new dimensions of support and joy to our lives. This openness has slowly transformed my approach to life and relationships, marking a phase of growth and new beginnings.

Empowering Our Children

When I think about empowering our children, I remember the discussions we had about the importance of open, honest communication and the profound role emotional intelligence plays in their development. Communicating effectively with our children sets a foundation for trust and understanding that extends far beyond the early years into adolescence and adulthood.

From my personal experience, I've learned that taking the time to truly listen to my children, to hear their thoughts and feelings without judgment, encourages them to open up and share more of their world with me. It's about creating a safe space where they feel valued and understood. This approach not only fosters a stronger bond but also builds their confidence to express themselves in the wider world.

I've often heard many parents wonder why their children don't trust them or open up to them. The common refrain is, "I'm their parent, not their friend." But I've come to believe that we must blend these roles effectively. Being a friend to our children, in addition to being a parent, can bridge gaps that traditional authoritative roles might widen. When we befriend our children, we show them that we respect their thoughts and are genuinely interested in their lives. This friendship fosters a deeper trust and makes it more likely that they will turn to us when they need advice or support, knowing they will be met with understanding rather than judgment. To be clear, my greatest responsibility and title is that of mother, and my children would vehemently state that I am the strictest parent in each of their friend circles. Befriending your children does not mean relaxing rules and discipline. It means that they are comfortable and feel safe to come to you with information that you'd rather know, to be able to discuss and advise, while reiterating expectations. This has been particularly beneficial during the tween and teen years.

Emotional intelligence is another key ingredient in empowering our children. By modeling empathy and teaching them to recognize and manage their emotions, we equip them with skills to navigate the complexities of relationships and challenges they will encounter. I make it a point to discuss emotions openly in our home, labeling them and talking through the feelings that arise from different situations. This has helped my children become more resilient and adaptable when things don't go their way.

Empowering our children also means stepping back at times to let them solve problems on their own. It can be tough to watch them struggle, but overcoming obstacles builds their strength and self-reliance. I encourage them to try new solutions, and I'm always here to guide them, not to take over. This balance is crucial for their growth and development.

I also believe in the power of encouragement and positive reinforcement. Celebrating their efforts and successes, big or small, boosts their self-esteem and motivates them to keep pushing forward. It's about letting them know that their efforts are appreciated and that they have the support they need to pursue their dreams.

In our journey together, remembering the importance of communication and emotional intelligence has been transformative. It has strengthened our relationship and empowered my children to face life's challenges with courage and optimism. I hope sharing my experience helps you feel more equipped and inspired to guide your children along their path to becoming confident, capable, and compassionate individuals.

PERSONAL SPACE: CREATING A SAFE AND HEALING HOME ENVIRONMENT

When I finally stepped away from a toxic relationship with a narcissist, one of the most healing actions I took was to create a safe, personal space for myself at home. This sanctuary became my foundation for rebuilding my life, piece by piece.

For anyone walking a similar path, I want to share why it's so crucial to cultivate a healing home environment. After experiencing the turmoil and emotional upheaval that comes with narcissistic abuse, the comfort of your own space can provide profound solace and security. It's in this personal haven where you can start to unravel the tangled emotions and begin the process of healing.

I focused on making my home a reflection of my inner desires and needs, something I had neglected for too long. I surrounded myself with colors that soothed me, filled spaces with books that inspired me, and personal mementos that reminded me of my journey and the resilient person I was becoming.

Next, I focused on incorporating elements of nature, which have a naturally healing effect. A few well-chosen plants brought life into my home, and their care routine helped establish a soothing daily practice. Even something as simple as a vase of fresh flowers or a collection of seashells can remind you of the beauty and rhythm of the natural world.

I also made it a priority to carve out a special corner just for reflection and meditation. This could be as simple as a comfortable chair by a window, a small altar with candles and inspirational quotes, or a space with your favorite books and a cozy blanket. This designated area became a physical symbol of my commitment to self-care and introspection.

Personalizing my space with art was another powerful tool for healing. Each selection reflected my personality and my identity, or meant a great deal to me, such as pieces created by my children. This personal expression helped me reconnect with aspects of myself that had been suppressed.

Creating this space wasn't just about physical comfort; it was about reclaiming my environment and, by extension, my mind and spirit. In this safe space, I allowed myself to feel every emotion—pain, joy, and eventually peace—without judgment. It became a physical manifestation of my newfound boundaries and self-respect.

A healing home is more than a shelter. It's a personal retreat where you can nurture your growth and gather strength. It's where you can experiment with who you are becoming without fear of criticism. Every small decision about decorating or utilizing the space reinforces your autonomy and decision-making power—skills often eroded in relationships with narcissists.

Creating Clarity: The Benefits of Decluttering Your Space

The act of decluttering can significantly reduce stress and anxiety. When our living spaces are cluttered, it creates chaos, which impacts our ability to focus and process information effectively (Stoler, 2023). By clearing out unnecessary items, we reduce the visual distractions that lead to cognitive overload. This simplification of our surroundings can lead to a calmer mind and a more focused state of being.

Moreover, decluttering is not just about improving mental clarity—it's also about emotional release. Messy environments can contribute to feelings of frustration, helplessness, and being overwhelmed. This emotional turbulence can often mirror the internal chaos we might feel after leaving a narcissistic relationship. By organizing our spaces, we address these heaps of disruption, which helps to calm our minds and soothe our spirits.

One profound benefit I noticed was an increase in energy and productivity. The less clutter there is, the less energy we expend managing it. This newfound energy can then be redirected toward more fulfilling activities that promote healing and growth.

Here's some guidance on how to start decluttering:

- **Start small:** Begin with manageable goals, such as tackling one drawer or one corner of a room. Doing this prevents the process from becoming overwhelming and builds momentum with each small success.
- **Emotional detachment:** For items that carry emotional weight but serve no current purpose, consider taking a photograph before letting them go. Doing this allows you to preserve the memory without clinging to the physical object.
- **Decide on disposal:** Make a plan for what to do with the items you choose to remove. Donating them can be a cathartic process, knowing that your unused

items will benefit someone else. This step can also reinforce feelings of generosity and connection, which are vital for emotional healing.

- **Ask for help:** If the process seems daunting, don't hesitate to enlist support from friends, family, or even a professional organizer. Sometimes, having an external perspective can make it easier to decide what stays and what goes (Stoler, 2023).

Creating a decluttered space is a powerful step toward healing. It reinforces your capacity to make decisions, reduces anxiety, and improves your overall well-being. Each cleared space can feel like a breath of fresh air, a small victory in reclaiming your life and moving forward with confidence and peace.

SECURING PEACE OF MIND: SAFETY MEASURES FOR YOUR SANCTUARY

Creating a sanctuary isn't just about comfort and aesthetics; it's also crucial to ensure that your home is a secure and safe environment. This aspect of home-making is especially important to me, as feeling safe brings a sense of peace that's foundational for healing and growth.

In my own journey, taking steps to secure my home helped alleviate the anxiety that lingered after leaving a turbulent relationship. Here are some practical measures I implemented to ensure my home felt both welcoming and secure:

- **Upgrade locks and secure entrances:** One of the first things I did was replace old locks with new, high-quality ones. This included the front and back doors and windows that were easily accessible. It's a straightforward step but significantly bolstered my sense of security.

- **Install a security system:** Depending on your budget and needs, consider installing a security system. There are many options available, from basic alarm systems to those with cameras, motion sensors, and 24-7 monitoring services. Knowing that my home was monitored gave me an added layer of reassurance.

- **Light up your landscape:** Well-lit exteriors can deter unwelcome visitors. Consider installing motion-sensor lights around the perimeter of your home, particularly in darker areas such as alleys or back entries. These lights are practical for security and make it safer to navigate outdoors at night.

- **Get to know your neighbors:** Building relationships with neighbors can create a supportive community and an extra set of eyes looking out for each other. I found comfort in knowing my neighbors were familiar with me and could recognize if something seemed amiss.

- **Maintain privacy:** While it's wonderful to have windows that let in natural light, it's also important to manage what can be seen from the outside. I chose window treatments that provided privacy at key times, particularly in the evenings. This way, I could enjoy the sunlight during the day without worrying about prying eyes at night.

- **Secure personal information:** In the digital age, home security also involves protecting your personal information. I ensured my Wi-Fi network was secure, used strong, unique passwords for online accounts, and was cautious about sharing personal details online.
- **Create a safety plan:** Finally, I developed a personal safety plan that included emergency contacts, a list of safe places, and an escape route in case of emergencies. Having this plan in place is a sobering reminder of the need for preparedness, but it's also incredibly empowering.

Implementing these safety measures has secured my home and fortified my mental and emotional well-being. Knowing I have taken proactive steps to protect myself helps me relax and enjoy the sanctuary I've created. It's about more than locks and lights; it's about crafting a space where you can thrive in tranquility and security.

EMBRACING SOLITUDE: FINDING PEACE IN BEING ALONE

There was a time when the idea of doing things alone felt somewhat daunting to me. The thought of going out solo, whether to a movie or a café, came with a tinge of embarrassment. But over time, I've discovered the profound difference between solitude and loneliness, and I've come to cherish the moments I spend by myself.

Solitude is not about being lonely; it's about enjoying and valuing your own company. It's an opportunity to connect with yourself on a deeper level, to engage in self-reflection, and to recharge in peace. Loneliness can feel empty and isolating, but solitude is enriching—it builds strength, peace, and independence.

I remember the first time I decided to go to the movies alone. Initially, I felt a bit self-conscious, but as I sat in the theater—choosing the exact spot I wanted, watching a film I picked out myself—I realized how liberating it felt. There was no need to compromise or worry about whether someone else was enjoying the movie. It was just me, my thoughts, and my full immersion in the experience.

Another joy I've embraced is treating myself to nice dinners or that occasionally overpriced coffee. There's something deeply satisfying about savoring a meal in quiet, without the need to make conversation or please anyone else but myself. It's a celebration of my own presence and preferences.

But, of all the solitary activities, sitting outdoors with a good book is by far my favorite. Whether I'm in my backyard or at the local park, these moments are my time to lose myself in my novels, people watch or enjoy music. The fresh air and the scenery help me to clear my mind and find new perspectives. These moments are a reminder that I am my own best companion in exploring the world.

For anyone new to spending time alone, start with something simple, like a walk or a coffee at your local café. Bring a book or journal if you like, or just sit and observe the world around you. You might find, as I did, that these moments of solitude become precious pockets of joy in your day.

Embracing solitude teaches us about our preferences, our thoughts, and our dreams. It's a practice of independence and self-affirmation. So, I encourage you to step out on your own sometimes. You might just discover that some experiences are not just manageable alone—they're actually more enjoyable.

PLANNING FOR THE FUTURE: SETTING GOALS AND DREAMING BIG

Finally, as we forge ahead in our journey to build a new life, it's essential to plan for the future. Reflecting on Chapter 3, we began to reclaim our self-identity and worth, setting goals that resonate with our true selves. We visualized these goals with a vision board and reignited our passions. Now, it's time to outline actionable steps to turn these goals into reality, setting clear timelines and defining milestones.

Setting realistic yet ambitious goals is a delicate balance. Start by asking yourself what you truly want to achieve in both your personal and professional life. These goals should stretch your capabilities but remain attainable. For instance, if you aim to change careers, start by enrolling in a course that enhances your skills. If your goal is to run a marathon, your first milestone could be to run a comfortable 5K.

Once you've set these goals, break them down into smaller, manageable tasks. Create a timeline for each task and establish milestones that will help you measure progress. For example, set a six-month goal to complete a certification course, with milestones for each module you complete.

Anticipating potential obstacles is also crucial. Challenges such as time constraints, financial limitations, or even self-doubt might arise. Plan for these by identifying possible solutions in advance. If time is an issue, could you perhaps wake up an hour earlier? If financial resources are limited, what budget adjustments could you make, or what financial aid could you seek?

Staying motivated can be tough, especially when progress seems slow or obstacles loom large. To maintain momentum, keep your vision board in a place where you see it daily. Remind yourself why these goals matter to you. Celebrate every small victory along the way—these milestones are proof of your progress. Perhaps keep a journal or blog about your journey, which can be a motivational tool to look back on and see how far you've come.

Also, cultivating a positive feedback loop can significantly enhance your self-perception and confidence. Develop practices that affirm and reinforce your achievements. For example, set aside time each week to reflect on what you've accomplished and write down three things you did well. This practice helps shift focus from what's pending to what's been achieved, reinforcing a sense of competence and control.

Remember, every achievement is a step closer to the life you envision. Celebrate these triumphs, no matter how small they might seem. Each one is a building block toward your larger dreams. Your goals are not just dreams; they are the blueprints for your future. Keep pushing forward, and don't forget to take moments to appreciate the journey and the growth you experience along the way.

As we close this chapter of our journey, we can see how much ground we've covered together. From embracing solitude to setting concrete goals, each step has been part of a larger journey toward building a new life.

Moving forward, the next chapter builds upon these foundations, focusing on maintaining our mental health and well-being. We will learn more about how managing stress, engaging in physical activity, and choosing the right nutrition can play pivotal roles in sustaining our health. We'll explore strategies to keep our minds clear and our bodies strong, ensuring we're equipped to handle whatever challenges come our way.

Just as we've learned to set goals and celebrate our progress, we'll learn to integrate these practices into a holistic approach to our health in the upcoming chapter. Keep this spirit of achievement alive as we continue to explore how best to support our total well-being in the chapter to come.

7

MAINTAINING MENTAL HEALTH
AND WELL-BEING

"Your mental health is a priority. Your happiness is an essential. Your self-care is a necessity."

— *MELODY BEATTIE*

Managing my stress and maintaining my mental health has been a journey marked by trial and error, and, ultimately, growth. While therapy played a significant role in my healing, and the unwavering support of my family and friends provided a foundation of love and encouragement, it was truly the holistic approach I adopted that made a lasting impact. This approach integrated routines involving physical activities, revamped eating habits, and lifelong practices that supported my overall well-being.

Incorporating regular physical activity into my daily life was one of the first steps I took. Whether it was walking the dog, a dance class, or jumping rope, moving my body became a crucial outlet for relieving stress. It wasn't just about keeping fit; it was about creating moments where I could step away from the mental clutter and find clarity. Each step, each stretch, brought me closer to peace.

Changing my eating habits was another key aspect. I learned that the foods I consumed could either be a source of comfort or a trigger for more stress. By choosing nutritious meals that fueled my body, I noticed a significant shift in my mood and energy levels. Integrating more fruits, vegetables, and whole grains and reducing processed foods helped stabilize my mood swings and kept me more balanced.

But beyond these physical aspects, it was the establishment of lifelong practices that truly anchored my mental health. Mindfulness and meditation became daily rituals. Taking time each day to sit quietly, breathe deeply, and center myself allowed me to face whatever challenges came with a sense of preparedness and poise. These practices didn't just help in moments of calm; they became lifelines in times of turmoil.

This holistic approach—balancing therapy, support, physical health, and mindful practices—helped me not just to manage stress but to transform how I interacted with the world around me. It taught me that taking care of my mind and body is not a luxury but a necessity.

For anyone struggling with stress or mental health, remember that finding what works for you might take time, and what works might be a blend of many different elements. In this chapter, we'll explore all these elements that helped me in my holistic health management. We'll explore the powerful interplay between physical activity, dietary choices, and mental wellness routines that have been pivotal in managing stress and enhancing overall well-being.

Together, we'll uncover practical tips and strategies to implement these practices in your own life, ensuring that you, too, can build a foundation of health that supports not just surviving but thriving.

MANAGING STRESS: LIFELONG PRACTICES FOR MENTAL WELL-BEING

We've explored a range of practices in our book, touching on mindfulness, journaling, creative pursuits, establishing routines, and the invaluable support from therapy and community groups. Each of these strategies has played a pivotal role in nurturing my mental well-being, especially during challenging times. Let me share how I've woven these practices into the fabric of my everyday life to manage stress and maintain mental clarity.

Mindfulness is a cornerstone of my daily routine. Whenever I catch myself feeling unfocused or caught in a loop of procrastination, I turn to the mindful techniques we discussed. By anchoring my attention to the present moment —whether through focused breathing or a mindful walk—I regain my sense of direction and purpose.

Journaling has been another lifeline. On days when my thoughts are a whirlwind and silence seems elusive, I sit down and pour everything onto the page. This process helps me organize my thoughts and prioritize my tasks, clearing the mental clutter and allowing me to focus on what truly matters.

Committing to a scheduled creative outlet, like my fifteen-minute yoga sessions, has been life-changing. Regardless of my mood, knowing I have dedicated this time to creativity gives me something to look forward to. Each session enhances my skills and reinforces my commitment to self-care—it's truly rewarding.

While therapy was a crucial step during my transition out of a difficult marriage, I've found that these ongoing practices, supported by a strong network of friends and family, now provide a robust foundation for my mental health.

Building on that foundation, understanding the specific stressors in my life and recognizing their triggers has been a game changer. By pinpointing exactly what sets off my stress responses—be it work deadlines, personal relationships, or even the pressure I put on myself—I've been able to craft targeted strategies to handle them more effectively. Learning how to identify these triggers early has helped me engage coping mechanisms (the strategies we learned) that prevent stress from escalating.

Furthermore, I've worked on sharpening my emotional regulation skills. It's one thing to recognize when you're stressed, but quite another to stay composed and constructive during those intense moments. Techniques such as deep breathing exercises, positive self-talk, and stepping back to reassess situations objectively have all empowered me to maintain my mental equilibrium even when the stakes are high.

And yet, we're not quite at the end of our journey. There are crucial aspects of my life I haven't yet shared, such as how I transformed my relationship with exercise, sleep, and food. These aren't just elements of my routine; they are integral to how I sustain my physical and mental health every single day.

THE ROLE OF PHYSICAL HEALTH IN EMOTIONAL RECOVERY

Sometimes, the simplest answers—exercise, sleep, and nutrition—seem too basic to be true solutions. When we're grappling with feelings of depression, anxiety, or stress, it's tempting to dismiss these fundamental health pillars in favor of more immediate relief. We often find ourselves at the doctor's office, hoping for medications or a quick fix that will "magically" cure us. While I acknowledge that medications can be beneficial and professional guidance is crucial, I also know from personal experience that making changes to these basic habits, though challenging at first, can work wonders for our health.

It's easy to overlook how profoundly our well-being is intertwined with how we move, sleep, and eat. Yet, embracing these essential aspects of health supports our physical condition and enhances our mental resilience, equipping us to better handle life's ups and downs.

Embracing Exercise for a Healthier Body and Mind

I've found that embracing regular physical activity is one of the most important steps I could take for my well-being. When I move my body, whether it's through yoga, walking, or any other form of exercise, I feel stronger not just physically but mentally as well. It's about more than just muscle; it's about resilience. Engaging in regular physical activities has been proven to enhance physical strength, endurance, bone density, and overall neuromusculoskeletal fitness (Mahindru et al., 2023). These benefits contribute massively to maintaining an independent, functional life as we age.

But the impact of exercise isn't limited to physical attributes. It profoundly affects our mental health too. Physical activity has a unique way of boosting mood and self-esteem while reducing stress. It's quite empowering to discover that regular movements can alter neurotransmitters in the brain, like endorphins and endocannabinoids, which are linked to feelings of happiness and decreased anxiety (Mahindru et al., 2023). Plus, the cognitive benefits are impressive—better focus, memory, and decision-making can follow a good workout.

One of the most crucial aspects of physical activity, for me, has been understanding and improving my body image. By focusing on what my body can do rather than how it looks, I've developed a more appreciative and positive view of myself. It's not about achieving a certain aesthetic; it's about feeling good, strong, and capable.

Finding the right type of exercise is key to making physical activity a regular part of your life. It's vital to discover what you enjoy—be it dancing, swimming, or cycling. When you love what you're doing, it doesn't feel like a chore; it becomes something you look forward to. This enjoyment is crucial because when exercise is a pleasure, it's easier to make it a consistent part of your routine.

Think about what makes you feel good. Do you prefer the quiet focus of yoga or the exhilarating rush of a spin class? Maybe you thrive on the precision and discipline of martial arts, or perhaps you find joy in the playful challenge of a team sport like basketball or soccer. There's a world of options out there, and the best choice is the one that brings a smile to your face.

It's also helpful to consider the social aspect of exercise. Some of us thrive on solitude, finding peace in the long run alone with our thoughts, while others get energized by the camaraderie and encouragement found in group classes or team settings. If you're unsure, try both! Join a class or invite a friend for a workout and see how the dynamics affect your experience.

Don't forget to listen to your body's cues. It's crucial to choose activities that not only excite you but also suit your body's needs. If you have joint concerns, swimming or an elliptical machine might be perfect for reducing strain. If you're dealing with stress or anxiety, rhythmic activities like rowing or running can be wonderfully meditative.

Lastly, keep your goals in sight, but be flexible in how you achieve them. Fitness isn't a one-size-fits-all journey. What matters is finding your path—one that keeps you motivated and feeling positive about the progress you're making. So grab your gear, step out the door, and start discovering what moves you. The most important step in your fitness journey is the next one you take.

Restful Nights: Cultivating Better Sleep for Better Health

The serenity and restoration that come from a good night's sleep are also closely tied to exercise. Engaging in physical activity helps regulate our sleep patterns, which is essential for both physical and mental recovery. Improved sleep quality further supports our health by enhancing immune function, reducing stress, and stabilizing our mood.

As someone who has navigated the challenges of restless nights, I've come to appreciate the critical role sleep plays in our overall health. Good sleep hygiene is a pivotal part of maintaining robust mental and emotional health. Studies have shown that improving sleep can significantly ameliorate issues like depression, anxiety, and even stress (Scott et al., 2021). It's clear that when we prioritize our sleep, we are also nurturing our mental well-being.

Here are some practical tips that have transformed my own sleep habits, and I hope they can help you, too:

- **Create a relaxing bedtime routine:** Start winding down an hour before bed. This could involve reading, gentle stretching, or a warm bath. The key is consistency; a predictable routine cues your body to prepare for sleep.
- **Optimize your sleep environment:** Make sure your bedroom is conducive to sleep—cool, quiet, and dark. Investing in blackout curtains and a comfortable mattress can make a big difference. Consider a white noise machine if external sounds are an issue.
- **Limit screen time:** The blue light emitted by screens can interfere with your ability to fall asleep. Try to disconnect from electronic devices at least an hour before bedtime.
- **Watch your intake:** Avoid caffeine and heavy meals close to bedtime. Both can disrupt your sleep cycle,

making it harder to fall asleep or causing you to wake up during the night.

- **Stick to a schedule:** Going to bed and waking up at the same time every day—even on weekends—can help regulate your body's internal clock and improve the quality of your sleep.
- **Mind your mindset:** Keep a sleep diary or engage in reflective journaling if you find yourself anxious or stressed at bedtime. This can help you unload your thoughts and clear your mind for a better night's rest.

Building a Healthy Relationship with Food

We've discussed the effects of physical exercise and the restorative benefits of sleep, but a good relationship with food cannot be overstated. To achieve holistic health, we need to consider these three elements—exercise, sleep, and nutrition—as foundational pillars supported by the other healthy practices we've learned.

For me, the journey to understanding my relationship with food has been pivotal. Counting calories, while effective for some, simply doesn't work for me. Instead, I've embraced the practice of intuitive eating. This approach involves listening to my body's hunger and fullness cues, eating when I'm truly hungry, and stopping when I'm comfortably full. It means trusting my body to make choices about food without adhering strictly to diets or eating schedules.

What's crucial in intuitive eating is a deep understanding of nutrition. It's about knowing what to avoid and what to embrace. For example, the common advice to reduce carb intake doesn't consider the essential role carbs play in our energy levels. Instead of cutting out carbs entirely, I've learned to distinguish between simple and complex carbohydrates. I avoid simple carbs, like sugar, that can lead to spikes and crashes in my blood sugar levels. Instead, I focus on complex carbs—whole grains, for instance—that provide sustained energy and support my body's needs, especially when breaking a fast.

Nutrition is not just about avoiding certain foods; it's about balance and understanding. While I follow intuitive eating principles, it's important to recognize that not all foods that seem healthy are equally beneficial. For example, not all fruits are created equal. Some have more complex sugars, which are better for maintaining energy levels throughout the day. This nuanced understanding of food helps me make informed choices that support both my physical and mental health.

Proteins are another essential part of my diet. Including a protein source in every meal helps me feel fuller for longer, significantly reducing my tendencies toward emotional eating or snacking out of boredom. This practice supports my mental health by stabilizing my mood and energy levels.

Understanding the impact of food on mental health has been eye-opening. Our brain is always on, managing everything from our heartbeat to our emotions, and it requires quality fuel to function optimally. Just like an expensive car, it performs best when it receives the best fuel—foods rich in vitamins, minerals, and antioxidants (Selhub, 2022). Diets high in refined sugars and processed foods can impair brain function and worsen symptoms of mood disorders, such as depression. This is because poor-quality nutrition can promote inflammation and oxidative stress, damaging brain cells and affecting our overall mood and cognitive functions.

The burgeoning field of nutritional psychiatry has shown how closely our diet is linked to our mental health. Interestingly, about 95% of serotonin—a key neurotransmitter regulating mood, sleep, and appetite—is produced in our gastrointestinal tract, which is heavily influenced by our gut bacteria. These bacteria play a critical role in our overall health, protecting our intestinal walls, reducing inflammation, and even affecting our mood and energy levels (Selhub, 2022).

By adopting a "clean" diet and reducing processed foods and sugars, I experienced a significant transformation in both my physical and emotional well-being. This shift in my lifestyle helped me appreciate the deep connection between my diet, physical health, and mental health.

Embracing a holistic approach to health—integrating balanced nutrition, regular physical activity, and adequate sleep—has been nothing short of life-changing. Each aspect of this approach supports and enhances the others, creating a synergy that uplifts my overall quality of life. I encourage you to consider how these interconnected practices can be tailored to fit your unique needs, building a foundation of well-being that supports every part of who you are.

CELEBRATING YOUR JOURNEY: REFLECTING ON HOW FAR YOU'VE COME

We've discussed the importance of celebrating our triumphs and the smaller victories along our path, but how do we put this into action? For me, after leaving a tumultuous situation, recognizing and honoring each step of personal growth became essential to my recovery and emotional well-being.

Incorporating gratitude practices into my daily life has profoundly shifted my perspective. Each morning, I take a moment to write down things I'm grateful for. It could be as simple as a sunny day, a friend's support, or a new skill I've learned. This practice centers my thoughts on positivity and growth, helping me focus on what I have gained rather than what I've left behind.

Creating traditions or rituals to mark personal milestones has also been a key part of my journey. For instance, on my children's birthdays, I take time to reflect on the year's progress. I might plant something new in my garden or buy a piece of art that resonates with our current state—something that symbolizes growth and renewal. These acts of celebration reinforce my accomplishments and remind me that change, though gradual, is always happening.

Sharing my story is another powerful tradition. It's a practice I've found to be profoundly healing, not just for myself, but also for those who listen. Each time I recount my experiences, I uncover a little more strength within myself, and perhaps offer some to others who might be struggling with similar issues.

Opening up about personal challenges and victories is not merely about unburdening oneself or seeking connection. It's about constructing a legacy of resilience and hope. By vocalizing our stories, we lay down stepping-stones for others to follow, showing them that recovery and happiness are attainable. Our experiences, especially the most painful ones, hold valuable lessons that, when shared, can significantly impact others' lives.

The act of sharing also empowers us by reaffirming our agency and our continuous progress on the path of healing. It transforms our most difficult moments into sources of strength for ourselves and for our community. This can create a supportive network that thrives on mutual understanding and encouragement.

Moreover, when we share our stories, we do more than narrate our past; we shape our identity and influence the narrative of recovery and personal growth. It reminds us— and those who hear us—that while our pasts are part of who we are, they do not have to dictate our future.

But our journey doesn't end here. As we turn the page to the next chapter, you will find affirmations for self-forgiveness, love, resilience, happiness, and success. These are potent tools for visualizing a positive future, setting realistic goals, and crafting the steps to achieve them. Combined with the knowledge and resilience we've cultivated so far, these techniques will empower you to harness your experiences and channel them into a fulfilling and thriving existence. Let's continue to build on our foundation, using every tool at our disposal.

8

AFFIRMATIONS FOR SELF-FORGIVENESS, LOVE, RESILIENCE, HAPPINESS, AND SUCCESS

"Everything will be okay in the end. If it's not okay, it's not the end."

— *JOHN LENNON*

When I first encountered the concept of affirmations, I was skeptical. The idea of repeating phrases to improve my mindset seemed, frankly, a bit simplistic. How could just saying something make it true? It wasn't until I really gave them a try that I began to see the subtle but profound shifts they could engender in my thoughts and feelings.

In Chapter 4, and throughout our journey together in this book, we've looked at the power of affirmations. You've learned how to craft your own personalized affirmations and discovered effective ways to weave them into your daily routine. This simple practice turned out to be transformative, helping reshape my self-perception and reality.

Now, in this final chapter, I am going to give you 100 affirmations, breaking them down into specific categories to make it easy for you to find the type of reassurance or boost you need at any given moment. Whether you're seeking a moment of empowerment or a reminder to forgive yourself, these affirmations will be your guide, helping to light the path forward on your journey of healing and growth. You can consider taking these one day at a time while working through the companion journal - "**100 Days of Affirmations: A Woman's Journey to Self-Forgiveness, Love, Resilience, Happiness and Success**" - to reflect more deeply on each. Start your day with each affirmation, and make time to reset throughout your day, by repeating it at various points. Place reminders in strategic locations or set an alarm on your phone to prompt you to pause for five minutes. After about three months of committing to speaking positivity into your life and affirming progress in various aspects, you can repeat the cycle or try generating new affirmations to reflect new goals.

SELF-LOVE AFFIRMATIONS: EMBRACING YOUR WORTH EVERY DAY

Self-love is not merely a state of feeling good. It is a profound acceptance of who you are and a commitment to nurturing your own growth and well-being. Here are some affirmations focused on fostering a deep and enduring love for oneself, designed to be repeated daily to reinforce a positive and loving mindset toward oneself.

1. I am worthy of love and respect. This affirmation is a cornerstone of self-love. It asserts your inherent value just as you are, without conditions. When repeated, it serves as a reminder that your worth is not contingent on external achievements or the approval of others.

2. I accept myself unconditionally. Many of us are our own harshest critics. This affirmation helps to soften the internal dialogue, promoting acceptance of all aspects of oneself, including perceived flaws and weaknesses.

3. I am enough. In a world that often pushes us to want more and to be more, this simple affirmation is a powerful antidote. It encourages contentment and self-acceptance, affirming that who you are right now is enough.

4. My mistakes are opportunities to learn and grow. This phrase shifts the perspective on failure from something to be avoided to something that is a natural part of the learning process. It fosters resilience by framing mistakes as steps toward personal growth.

5. I give myself permission to take care of my needs. Self-care is a fundamental aspect of self-love. This affirmation emphasizes the importance of looking after your own needs, reminding you that caring for yourself is not selfish but necessary.

6. I am proud of how far I've come. Recognizing and celebrating your own progress is crucial in the journey of self-love. This affirmation helps you to acknowledge your achievements and the growth that you have experienced.

7. I deserve to be happy and content. This affirmation counters feelings of unworthiness and guilt that can often accompany the pursuit of personal happiness. It asserts your right to seek out joy and contentment in life.

8. I honor my boundaries and insist others respect them. Maintaining healthy boundaries is a key aspect of self-love. This affirmation reinforces the importance of setting and enforcing boundaries that protect your emotional and physical well-being.

9. I choose to surround myself with positive and supportive people. Who you choose to spend time with can significantly affect your self-esteem and emotional health. This affirmation encourages you to choose relationships that uplift and support you.

10. I trust myself to make the best decisions for me. Self-trust is an essential component of self-love. This affirmation fosters confidence in your ability to make decisions that are right for you.

11. I am a work in progress, and that's okay. Embracing the concept of being a "work in progress" can alleviate a lot of self-imposed pressure. This affirmation promotes patience and the understanding that personal growth is an ongoing journey.

12. I let go of self-judgment and embrace self-compassion. Moving from judgment to compassion is a transformative process. This affirmation helps to cultivate a gentler and more compassionate attitude toward oneself.

13. I am deserving of my dreams and goals. Believing in your worthiness to achieve your dreams is crucial. This affirmation bolsters the belief that you deserve to pursue and achieve whatever you dream of.

14. I radiate beauty, charm, and grace. This helps enhance your self-image and confidence by affirming your inner and outer beauty.

SELF-FORGIVENESS AFFIRMATIONS: EMBRACING COMPASSION AND RELEASE

Self-forgiveness is a vital part of emotional healing and personal growth. It involves releasing past regrets and embracing the opportunity to move forward with greater wisdom and kindness toward oneself. Here are some carefully crafted affirmations that focus on nurturing self-forgiveness, helping you to let go of self-blame and cultivate a more forgiving attitude toward yourself.

15. I forgive myself for past mistakes. This affirmation acknowledges that making mistakes is part of being human and emphasizes the importance of forgiving oneself to move forward.

16. I release my past and live fully in the present. Holding onto past errors can hinder your present happiness. This affirmation helps you let go and focus on living in the moment.

17. I am learning and growing every day. This phrase reaffirms that every experience, good or bad, contributes to your growth, underscoring that learning is a continuous journey.

18. Every day, I grow stronger and more compassionate with myself. Emphasizing progress in self-compassion, this affirmation promotes the daily strengthening of your forgiving nature toward yourself.

19. I allow myself to move beyond guilt and embrace peace. Guilt can be consuming; this affirmation encourages the release of guilt and the acceptance of inner peace.

20. I accept that I did the best I could at the time with what I knew. This affirmation helps put past actions into perspective, fostering understanding and forgiveness toward oneself.

21. I honor my journey and my process of becoming. This celebrates your life's path, including all the twists and turns, acknowledging that each step is part of becoming who you are meant to be.

22. I choose to forgive myself and set myself free. Forgiveness is a choice that can lead to freedom from past burdens, and this affirmation empowers you to make that choice.

23. My mistakes are not a reflection of my worth. This affirmation separates your intrinsic worth from your actions, reinforcing that your value as a person is not diminished by errors.

24. I am worthy of forgiveness from myself and others. This phrase reinforces the idea that everyone deserves forgiveness, including you, from yourself and those around you.

RESILIENCE AFFIRMATIONS: STRENGTHENING YOUR INNER FORTITUDE

Resilience is the remarkable ability to bounce back from challenges and adversity, an essential quality for personal growth and emotional well-being. Cultivating resilience helps you navigate the ups and downs of life with greater ease and confidence. Here are some affirmations designed to build and reinforce your resilience, enabling you to face life's challenges with strength and poise.

25. I adapt to change with flexibility and grace. Change is inevitable, and this affirmation encourages a positive and adaptable response, helping you to navigate transitions smoothly.

26. I am strong enough to face life's challenges. This powerful statement reinforces your inner strength, boosting your confidence to tackle any obstacle.

27. Challenges are opportunities to grow and learn. By reframing difficulties as opportunities, this affirmation helps you approach problems with a proactive and positive mindset.

28. I am resilient, capable, and strong. This is a reminder of your inherent strength and capability, bolstering your self-belief in tough times.

29. Every setback teaches me valuable lessons. Recognizing the lessons in every setback can transform challenges into invaluable learning experiences.

30. I bounce back from disappointment with renewed strength. This affirmation fosters a resilient mindset that quickly recovers from setbacks and is ready to face new challenges.

31. My resilience grows stronger with each challenge I overcome. It's a reminder that resilience builds cumulatively, strengthened by each experience.

32. I am supported by others and the universe in my journey. Recognizing external support can enhance feelings of security and resilience.

33. I let go of what I cannot change and focus on what I can influence. This affirmation encourages practicality and a focus on actionable steps, which is crucial for resilience.

34. I am patient with myself as I navigate through difficult periods. Patience is a virtue that can significantly aid resilience, allowing time for recovery and adjustment without self-judgment.

35. My spirit is unbreakable, even by the toughest of challenges. This is a strong statement that underlines the indomitable nature of the human spirit.

36. I am a survivor, not a victim. This phrase shifts the narrative from passivity to active survival and overcoming, empowering you to take control of your life narrative.

37. My challenges do not define me; they refine me. This affirmation highlights growth and improvement through challenges rather than being defined or limited by them.

HAPPINESS AFFIRMATIONS: CULTIVATING JOY IN DAILY LIFE

Happiness is a state that many aspire to reach and maintain. It involves an attitude of appreciation for life's blessings and a positive mindset that can transform everyday experiences. Here are some affirmations aimed at nurturing happiness within yourself, allowing you to embrace joy and spread it to others.

38. I choose to focus on the positives in my life. This affirmation helps you consciously direct your attention to the good things in your life, fostering a habit of gratitude and positivity.

39. Joy flows through me with every breath I take. Encourages a deep connection with joy at a physical level, reminding you that happiness can be a natural state of being.

40. I am responsible for my own happiness. Emphasizes personal responsibility for happiness, empowering you to create joy regardless of external circumstances.

41. Each day brings wonderful new surprises. Opens your mind to the potential for joy and excitement each new day can bring, encouraging a sense of anticipation and curiosity.

42. I am grateful for every moment that life offers. Gratitude is a powerful enhancer of happiness, and this affirmation helps cultivate a thankful attitude toward life's many experiences.

43. Laughter and joy are abundant in my life. Highlights the presence and importance of laughter and joy, affirming their abundance in your life.

44. I find reasons to smile every day. Encourages the recognition and appreciation of daily moments that bring joy and contentment.

45. I allow myself to enjoy each moment. By giving yourself permission to fully enjoy each moment, you enhance your ability to experience happiness more deeply.

46. My heart is light; I am at ease. Promotes a sense of lightness and relaxation, which are conducive to experiencing happiness.

47. I celebrate life's joys, no matter how big or small. Encourages celebration of all joys, recognizing that happiness often lies in the small, everyday moments.

48. I let go of worries and embrace peace. Helps reduce anxiety and stress by promoting a focus on inner peace, which supports a happy mindset.

49. Every day, I discover more things to be happy about. Keeps the mind actively engaged in seeking out new joys, reinforcing a positive outlook on life.

50. I am content with who I am and what I have. Cultivates contentment, an important aspect of happiness, by appreciating oneself and one's circumstances.

51. I find humor in life and laugh often. Highlights the importance of humor as a source of happiness and resilience.

52. My life is filled with happiness, and I share it freely with others. Not only does it acknowledge the presence of happiness in your life, but also emphasizes the joy in sharing it with others.

SUCCESS AFFIRMATIONS: MANIFESTING ACHIEVEMENT AND PROSPERITY

Success is often a journey marked by persistence, learning, and growth. These affirmations are crafted to inspire a mindset focused on achievement, helping you harness your potential and realize your goals. Whether in your career, personal projects, or day-to-day activities, these positive statements reinforce your ability to succeed.

53. I am capable of achieving great things. This affirmation instills confidence in your abilities and potential, setting a foundation for pursuing ambitious goals.

54. Every day, I move closer to my dreams. This gentle reminder helps you see daily progress as a step toward fulfilling your biggest aspirations.

55. I am a magnet for success because of my dedication and commitment. Acknowledges that your hard work and dedication are powerful attractors for success.

56. My actions create constant prosperity. This statement reinforces the idea that the actions you take have a direct impact on your success and prosperity.

57. I am surrounded by abundance. Encourages a mindset that recognizes and appreciates abundance in all forms, enhancing your ability to attract more.

58. I excel in all that I do, and success comes naturally to me. Affirms your competence and natural ability to excel, fostering an environment where success is inevitable.

59. I am innovative and open to new ideas that can bring about success. Highlights your openness to innovations and new strategies that can lead to success.

60. I set clear goals and work to surpass them. This affirmation underlines the importance of setting specific, measurable goals and the drive to exceed them.

61. I am grateful for my success and the success of others. Cultivates a positive attitude toward your own achievements and those of others, fostering a supportive and abundant environment.

62. Every setback is a setup for a comeback. Turns challenges into opportunities, promoting resilience and the ability to bounce back stronger from setbacks.

63. I trust my intuition and wisdom to guide me to the right decisions. Strengthens trust in your own judgment and decision-making processes, essential for navigating the path to success.

64. I am respected in my field, and my expertise is valued. Affirms your professional stature and the value of your contributions, boosting your confidence and authority.

65. I am constantly learning and evolving. Emphasizes continuous personal and professional development as key components of success.

66. My mind is clear, focused, and equipped for success. Ensures mental clarity and focus, which are crucial for achieving goals.

67. I inspire and empower others to achieve their success. Recognizes your role in supporting and inspiring others, which can also amplify your own success.

68. I navigate challenges with ease and confidence. Prepares you to handle obstacles confidently, ensuring they do not derail your path to success.

69. I am a leader in my area, continuously pushing the boundaries of what is possible. Positions you as an innovator and leader, someone who actively shapes the field and creates new opportunities.

HEALTH AFFIRMATIONS: CULTIVATING WELLNESS FOR ALL AGES

Maintaining health and fostering a nurturing environment for ourselves and our children is fundamental to a life filled with vitality and joy. These affirmations focus on promoting personal health and encouraging a positive, health-focused mindset for children. They are designed to reinforce healthy habits, boost self-esteem related to health, and ensure a nurturing atmosphere for growth and wellness.

70. I honor my body by treating it with care and respect. This affirmation encourages a respectful and caring attitude toward your own body, emphasizing the importance of self-care.

71. I am attuned to the needs of my body and nourish it accordingly. This statement fosters a mindful relationship with your body, helping you to listen to and respond to its needs appropriately.

72. Every cell in my body vibrates with energy and health. Visualizes health at a cellular level, affirming robust energy and wellness throughout the body.

73. I am committed to learning about and living a healthy lifestyle. Encourages continuous learning and dedication to healthy living, which is crucial for long-term health.

74. I choose to make positive health choices that improve my well-being. Affirms the power of choice in health, emphasizing that you are in control of selecting beneficial practices.

75. I feel stronger and healthier with each passing day. A motivational affirmation that highlights progressive improvement in health and strength.

76. I teach my children the importance of healthy eating and exercise. Focuses on the role of parents in guiding children toward healthy habits that will last a lifetime.

77. My children's bodies are strong, capable, and healthy. Reinforces the idea of strength and capability in children, boosting their confidence in their own bodies.

78. We enjoy being active as a family. Encourages family activities that promote health and togetherness, reinforcing healthy habits through shared experiences.

79. I create a loving, healthy environment for my children. Emphasizes the parent's role in crafting an atmosphere that supports the overall well-being of children.

80. My children learn to love their bodies and care for them with joy. Teaches children body positivity and the joy found in caring for oneself.

81. We speak positively about health and our bodies, setting a foundation for lifelong wellness. Fosters a positive dialogue about health and body image, which is essential in building a healthy self-image in children.

82. My children understand the importance of rest and rejuvenation. Teaches children the value of rest and ensures they understand its role in maintaining health.

83. I empower my children with knowledge about health, allowing them to make informed choices. Encourages educating children about health, giving them the tools to make decisions that benefit their well-being.

PEACE AND CALM AFFIRMATIONS: CULTIVATING SERENITY IN EVERYDAY LIFE

In a world that often feels chaotic and stressful, finding moments of peace and calm is essential for maintaining mental and emotional well-being. These affirmations are crafted to help instill a sense of tranquility within yourself, allowing you to navigate daily stresses with ease and maintain a serene outlook.

84. Peace begins within me; I choose serenity over chaos. This affirmation empowers you to choose your response to external circumstances, reinforcing that peace is a personal state that can be cultivated regardless of the environment.

85. With each breath I take, I invite calmness into my body. Breathing consciously is a powerful tool for calming the mind and body; this affirmation helps focus on using breath to achieve tranquility.

86. My mind is clear, my heart is tranquil, and my body is at rest. A comprehensive affirmation that promotes peace across all dimensions of your being—mental, emotional, and physical.

87. I release tension with every exhale and feel more relaxed with every inhale. Encourages the physical release of stress and the renewal of energy with breathing, enhancing feelings of relaxation.

146 | NARCISSISTIC ABUSE RECOVERY

88. I embrace quiet moments to connect with my inner peace. Highlights the importance of taking breaks to foster inner peace, suggesting that solitude can be rejuvenating.

89. Serenity flows through me like a gentle river. Evokes imagery of a smooth, flowing river, symbolizing a steady and uninterrupted state of calm.

90. I let go of worries and embrace the present moment. Focuses on mindfulness, encouraging the release of past or future concerns to fully engage with the here and now.

91. Calmness washes over me with every situation I face. Instills confidence that you can maintain composure and peace, even in challenging situations.

92. I am detached from external pressures; my inner peace is unshaken. Promotes emotional resilience by detaching from external stresses and maintaining a core of stability.

93. My environment reflects my peaceful intentions. Affirms that your surroundings can be crafted to reflect and enhance your inner peace, promoting a harmonious living space.

94. Every day, I grow more at peace with myself and the world. Affirms continuous improvement in personal peace, suggesting that this is an evolving quality that deepens over time.

95. Tranquility is my natural state; I return to it easily. Reinforces that peace is inherent and accessible, emphasizing ease in returning to a state of calm.

96. I am grounded and peaceful, no matter the chaos around me. Encourages a strong sense of grounding, suggesting that internal peace can be maintained despite external disorder.

97. I use silence as a shield against life's noise. Highlights the power of silence as a tool to protect against overstimulation, promoting quiet as a resource for maintaining peace.

98. I am in harmony with the universe, which brings peace to my spirit. Suggests a spiritual dimension to peace, aligning personal serenity with a larger cosmic order.

99. Stress flows out of my body naturally and effortlessly. Encourages the natural expulsion of stress, promoting a physical and metaphorical release of tension.

100. I find peace in letting things be without the need for control. Emphasizes acceptance and the release of control as pathways to peace, suggesting that peace comes from trust and letting go.

I hope these affirmations resonate with you as deeply as they have with me, guiding you toward greater self-love, forgiveness, resilience, happiness, success, health, peace, and empowerment. Remember, the power of these affirmations lies not merely in their repetition but in the belief we invest in them. Let them be your daily companions, whispering words of encouragement and transformation as you navigate the complexities of life. You're committing to a practice of positive change, crafting a reality that reflects your true potential by embracing these affirmations. Carry them close to your heart and watch as they help unfold a life rich with growth and fulfillment.

CONCLUSION

> *"You are braver than you believe, stronger than you seem, and smarter than you think."*
>
> — *A.A. MILNE*

Reflecting on the journey you've been on through the pages of this book, you should be deeply moved by your resilience and strength. You've taken huge steps toward healing from narcissistic abuse, steps that have begun to rebuild your self-worth and independence. This process isn't easy, and your commitment to navigating this path is truly commendable.

Throughout our time together, we've explored crucial aspects of recovery. We've delved into understanding the nature of narcissistic abuse, processing the grief that comes with it, and reclaiming the self-identity that was overshadowed by another's manipulation. You've learned practical tools for healing and ways to foster resilience. We've discussed establishing healthy relationships and the empowering process of building a new life founded on independence and self-respect.

A few core messages have underpinned our discussions: the critical importance of self-care, the power of setting boundaries, the strength that can be found in allowing yourself to be vulnerable, and the courage required to trust again. These are not just concepts but practical approaches to carry with you as you move forward.

As you continue on this journey of self-discovery and personal development, I encourage you to keep visualizing a positive future and putting into practice the realistic goals you've set for yourself. Remember, healing is an ongoing process. Setbacks are simply part of the journey, not endpoints. They offer valuable lessons that, when embraced, propel you further along the path to a more fulfilled life.

To aid in your continuous healing, I've crafted a companion journal titled "100 Days of Affirmations: A Woman's Journey to Self-Forgiveness, Love, Resilience, Happiness and Success." Each day focuses on a specific affirmation from this book, encouraging daily reflection and deeper exploration of your thoughts and feelings. This journal is a tool to document your progress, reflect on the affirmations that resonate with you, and explore new insights as they arise.

You are not alone in this journey. There's a community of survivors who share your experiences and support each other in healing. Sharing your own story can be incredibly empowering, not just for you but for others who are navigating similar paths. Consider joining support groups, participating in workshops, or simply reaching out to a trusted friend to continue building your support network.

Thank you for trusting me to guide you through such a personal and transformative process. Your courage in facing your past, your commitment to your healing journey, and your trust in these words have been nothing short of inspiring. Always remember your inherent worth and the bright future that awaits you. Embrace tomorrow with optimism, equipped with the tools, knowledge, and resilience you've gained. Here's to your continued growth and a life filled with peace, joy, and empowerment.

> *"In the midst of winter, I found there was, within me, an invincible summer."*

— *ALBERT CAMUS*

REFERENCES

Arabi, S. (2024, January 16). *Narcissists cause cognitive dissonance – here's how to destroy it, for good.* Thought Catalog. https://thoughtcatalog.com/shahida-arabi/2023/02/narcissists-cause-cognitive-dissonance-heres-how-to-destroy-it-for-good/

Cuncic, A. (2023, November 6). *Effects of narcissistic abuse.* Verywell Mind. https://www.verywellmind.com/effects-of-narcissistic-abuse-5208164

Day, N. J., Townsend, M. L., & Grenyer, B. F. (2021, November 16). Pathological narcissism: An analysis of interpersonal dysfunction within intimate relationships. *Personality and Mental Health, 16*(3), 204–216. https://doi.org/10.1002/pmh.1532

Gibson, J. (2019, September 13). Mindfulness, interoception, and the body: A contemporary perspective. *Frontiers in Psychology, 10.* https://doi.org/10.3389/fpsyg.2019.02012

Holland, K. (2023, May 17). *The stages of grief: How to understand your feelings.* Healthline. https://www.healthline.com/health/stages-of-grief

Hurley, K. (2024, February 17). *What is resilience? your guide to facing life's challenges, adversities, and crises.* EverydayHealth. https://www.everydayhealth.com/wellness/resilience/

Laderer, A. (2023, November 10). *Therapy that will actually help you heal from narcissistic abuse.* Charlie Health. https://www.charliehealth.com/post/what-is-the-best-therapy-for-narcissistic-abuse

Landers, J. (2012, July 25). *Seven must-do steps for women who want financial stability post-divorce.* Forbes. https://www.forbes.com/sites/jefflanders/2012/07/25/seven-must-do-steps-for-women-who-want-financial-stability-post-divorce/?sh=5bcf84656ec2

March, E., Kay, C. S., Dinić, B. M., Wagstaff, D., Grabovac, B., & Jonason, P. K. (2023, June 23). "It's All in your head": Personality traits and gaslighting tactics in intimate relationships. *Journal of Family Violence.* https://doi.org/10.1007/s10896-023-00582-y

Mahindru, A., Patil, P., & Agrawal, V. (2023, January 7). Role of physical activity on mental health and well-being: A Review. *Cureus.* https://doi.org/10.7759/cureus.33475

Mayo Clinic Staff. (2023, August 1). *Chronic stress puts your health at risk.*

Mayo Clinic. https://www.mayoclinic.org/healthy-lifestyle/stress-management/in-depth/stress/art-20046037

Scott, A. J., Webb, T. L., Martyn-St James, M., Rowse, G., & Weich, S. (2021, October 2). Improving sleep quality leads to better mental health: A meta-analysis of randomised controlled trials. *Sleep Medicine Reviews, 60,* 101556. https://doi.org/10.1016/j.smrv.2021.101556

Selhub, E. (2022, September 18). *Nutritional psychiatry: Your brain on food.* Harvard Health. https://www.health.harvard.edu/blog/nutritional-psychiatry-your-brain-on-food-201511168626

Shukla, A., Choudhari, S. G., Gaidhane, A. M., & Quazi Syed, Z. (2022, August 15). Role of art therapy in the promotion of Mental Health: A Critical Review. *Cureus.* https://doi.org/10.7759/cureus.28026

Stoler, D. R. (2023, February 15). *The many mental benefits of decluttering.* Psychology Today. https://www.psychologytoday.com/intl/blog/the-resilient-brain/202302/the-many-mental-benefits-of-decluttering

Wakefield, M. (2023, July 27). *The cycle of narcissistic abuse.* Narcissistic Abuse Rehab. https://www.narcissisticabuserehab.com/cycle-of-narcissistic-abuse/

Printed in Great Britain
by Amazon